THE COMPLETE
GLUTEN-FREE
VEGAN COOKBOOK

THE COMPLETE GLUTEN-FREE VEGAN COOKBOOK

125 Recipes Everyone Can Enjoy

Justin Weber

Photography by Marija Vidal

ROCKRIDGE
PRESS

Interior and Cover Designer: Lisa Forde
Art Producer: Sara Feinstein
Editor: Cecily McAndrews
Production Editor: Andrew Yackira

Photography © 2021 Marija Vidal. Food styling by Elisabet der Nederlanden.

ISBN: Print 978-1-64876-662-6 | eBook 978-1-64876-161-4
R1

This book goes out
to my grandmas,
Helen and Gloria,
who taught me how to
love through food.

Cinnamon Rolls,
page **42**

Contents

Introduction

FOOD HAS ALWAYS BEEN A PART OF MY STORY. My mom was a wedding cake baker, my grandfather a chef at a local German restaurant, and my grandmother famous for her apple pie, and I watched and helped and soaked it all in. I learned early that food is a way to welcome others, to create memories, and to celebrate traditions and one another.

But in a world full of social media accounts featuring delicious-looking foods that may not fit your food preferences or needs, it can be a challenge to be excited by and celebrate with food. My goal with this book is to create a resource for anyone who chooses to eat vegan and gluten-free meals, so that everyone feels welcome at the table.

Food products and restaurant food almost always have gluten in them or sneaky little non-vegan-friendly ingredients. (Gelatin, I'm talking to you!) Not so in this book. All 125 of these recipes are gluten-free, vegan, flavorful, colorful, and designed for *everyone.* No need to scrutinize any ingredient lists, and no need for a culinary background, either. If you feel limited by your gluten-free, vegan diet, my hope is that this book will open you to an entire world of good-looking, great-tasting options.

This book explores a variety of different gluten-free flours and nondairy milks, includes unique spice blends for flavoring all sorts of dishes, and offers useful advice for getting the most out of plant-based proteins. The recipes cover every eating occasion, from basics to breakfast, special occasion mains to desserts.

As you journey through this collection of gluten-free, vegan recipes, you will gain a deeper appreciation of food through a variety of ingredients, tips and tricks, and styles so you can welcome everyone to your table. Food is love, and I'm honored to share these meals with you.

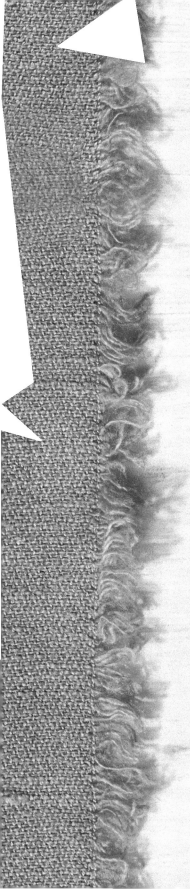

HOW THIS BOOK WORKS

If you are new to gluten-free and vegan cooking, you might feel a little (or a lot) of anxiety about getting started. Much of Western-style cooking is dominated by wheat and animal products, which can be disheartening. As a salve for that anxiety, this first chapter gives you the foundational information you'll need to better understand gluten-free and vegan cooking for yourself or for loved ones.

After you've covered the basics, you'll feel prepared to move into the recipe chapters, which offer a wide variety of styles of food to show off how amazing gluten-free, vegan food can be. The recipe chapters begin with breakfasts like Carrot Cake Donuts (page 32). Then, the book moves on to cover snacks and sides like Cheesy Bowtie Crackers (page 57) and Brussels Sprout Slaw (page 97) that can accompany your lunch of Eggplant Bacon "E-L-T" (page 78) or whatever else piques your interest. From there, you can move on to explore dinners like Tempeh Tacos (page 136) before enjoying desserts, such as Flourless Chocolate Cake (page 176).

It's a great idea to read each recipe twice before starting, just in case there are some unfamiliar ingredients or techniques or time requirements that could alter your planning. To build your confidence, all of the recipes have labels at the top to let you know if they are soy-free, nut-free, whole-food plant-based, a crowd-pleaser, or, maybe best of all, doable in under 30 minutes. Additionally, many of the recipes include tips that offer you more information on an ingredient or technique, a variation, or a way to make some of it in advance.

CHAPTER 1

The Gluten-Free Vegan Kitchen

WELCOME TO THE WORLD of gluten-free and vegan cooking. The first step to learning how to cook this way is to develop an understanding of how gluten-free and vegan ingredients work. This is the most exciting part of the book, because you'll learn that a gluten-free and vegan lifestyle doesn't mean compromise or sacrifice. Rather, it means opportunity—opportunity to learn more about food and to experience meals and ingredients that will completely transform how you think about recipes and your pantry.

6 Reasons Gluten-Free and Vegan Is Great

Eating a gluten-free and vegan diet does not mean sacrificing flavor, comfort, heritage, or the enjoyment of food. It is clear by the rising number of gluten-free and vegan choices at restaurants and stores that there's a market for it, and that people are literally hungry for a variety of food options. Here are some of the many benefits of a gluten-free, vegan lifestyle:

1. The Heart of Nutrition: Replacing animal-based products with plant-based ones dramatically lowers your risk for heart disease. Animal products are high in cholesterol and saturated fats, whereas plants provide a variety of vitamins and minerals as well as fiber and phytonutrients.

2. Pain-Free Movement: For those with celiac disease or gluten intolerance, even the smallest amount of gluten, as little as a crouton, can cause a range of problems that negatively affect comfort, mobility, and their general sense of well-being. Cutting out gluten can also reduce the joint pain associated with inflammation.

3. Better Complexion: Gluten and dairy are known to trigger an inflammatory response that often causes skin conditions like acne or eczema. Plus, the hormones in dairy can cause an increase in pore-clogging oil production in your skin. After eliminating or limiting gluten and dairy, you may see dramatic changes in your complexion.

4. Less Water Pollution: Raising cows for meat or dairy takes a lot of water. It takes over ten times the amount of water to raise an average cow than it does to grow the same weight in grain. Animal farming is also a huge contributor to water pollution due to the resulting runoff of animal waste, antibiotics, and hormones. Going vegan or limiting the use of animal products in your lifestyle helps reduce your water footprint.

5. Cleaner Eating: Cooking gluten-free and vegan foods introduces you to ingredients that are fresh and mostly unprocessed. Most processed foods, unless specifically labeled otherwise, contain wheat and animal products. When you cook with fresh, whole foods, the quality of your meals improves because you're using higher-quality ingredients.

6. Increased Energy: It takes extra energy for your body to digest meat and dairy products. On the other hand, whole foods like fruits, veggies, and whole grains contain lots of nutrients, give you energy, and keep you feeling satisfied rather than sluggish and overly full.

Stocking Your Kitchen

The quality of the food you make depends on the ingredients you make it with. But don't worry, that doesn't mean you have to tap into your 401(k) to buy ingredients or hunt through the forest for morel mushrooms. In this section, you'll learn about the simple, essential ingredients of gluten-free, vegan cooking.

Gluten-Free Flours

It's important to understand what gluten is exactly and where it comes from. Gluten is the generic name for the proteins present in wheat, rye, and barley. Those who are gluten intolerant, sensitive, or allergic are affected by the prolamins, or proteins, in these grains. These proteins are what gives wheat-based products their shape, chew, and elastic texture. Gluten-free flours do not contain these proteins, so they are often paired with other ingredients like xanthan gum, agar, and starches in recipes to create a similar result. Throughout this book you will use a variety of gluten-free flours for breads, batters, and cakes. Here are some of my favorites:

GLUTEN-FREE ALL-PURPOSE BLENDS
These blends are often a mix of rice flours, starches, sorghum, and a gum or binder like xanthan. Every brand has its own variations, with varying results. I usually use my own blend (page 206) because it's easy to make and affordable, and it gives me the most consistent results. You will be using gluten-free all-purpose flour often throughout this book, and a five-pound bag will get

you through most of the recipes. If you prefer to buy it premade, I recommend Bob's Red Mill Gluten-Free 1 to 1 Baking Flour or King Arthur Baking Company's Gluten-Free Measure for Measure Flour.

OAT FLOUR

Oats on their own are gluten-free, because they do not have the prolamins that trigger gluten allergies and sensitivities. Nonetheless, oats are often grown next to wheat and rye or processed using the same equipment, leading to cross-contamination. Look for the gluten-free label on oat flour or oats if you have a gluten allergy. Oat flour is mild in flavor and gives a fluffy texture to pancakes and waffles.

OTHER FLOURS

Almond flour has become a popular gluten-free option because it has a slight nutty flavor and offers the same nutritional benefits as eating almonds; however, it can be dense and slightly gritty, so always be sure to use finely ground flour. **Coconut flour** is gluten-free, low carb, and low calorie. However, it can also be very dense, and, well, it tastes like coconut. You should use about 75 percent less coconut flour than the amount of all-purpose flour called for in a recipe. Both almond and coconut flours should be blended with another flour to lighten their consistencies and flavors. Despite its name, **buckwheat flour** is not part of the wheat family and does not contain gluten. It lends its nutty flavor to baked goods, but it does not provide structure; you'll need to add stabilizers like xanthan gum or starch to hold buckwheat breads and other treats together.

Dairy Alternatives

The variety of available dairy alternatives has rapidly expanded in the past few years as more people have discovered the nutritional and health benefits of cutting dairy from their diets. Dairy contains high levels of saturated fats and hormones that lead to a variety of health complications. Below are a few dairy alternatives for gluten-free and vegan recipes. If you'd like to make your own nondairy milk, see pages 218 to 219 in the Basics chapter.

COCONUT MILK

There are two main types of coconut milk that you can find in stores: canned and boxed. Canned coconut milk, generally found in the international section of the market, is thicker and contains more fat than the boxed variety that's sold on the health food shelves. Canned coconut milk is labeled according to the amount of natural fat and sweetness it contains. Choosing a type depends on the recipe. Baked goods can use the boxed style, but desserts and curry sauces benefit from the added fat in the can for texture and flavor.

ALMOND MILK

Almond milk is sold both in the refrigerator section and on shelves in the health food sections of grocery stores. The refrigerated version is often thicker and contains fewer preservatives, but both can be used for baked goods. Almond milk is not recommended for savory sauces because of the slight natural sweetness that can be off-putting in savory foods.

OAT MILK

Oat milk has gained popularity in recent years, thanks to coffee shop baristas. Its thick texture and ability to make foam makes it a great alternative for lattes and other coffee drinks. It is also the best nondairy, gluten-free milk for savory sauces because of its neutral flavor and thick consistency. If you're allergic to gluten, it's important to check oat milk labels for cross-contamination or make your own (see page 218).

Oils and Fats

Fat is a necessary macronutrient that aids in digestion, brain health, and vitamin absorption. There are many vegan oils and fats that are wonderful for baking, and many big brands like Country Crock now offer nondairy butters. When baking, fat is vital for stability, light texture, and color.

VEGAN BUTTER

Nondairy butter has taken over the grocery shelves, with many brands offering baking sticks, spreads, and even European-style cultured butters. The most popular brand of vegan butter is Earth Balance, which produces both soy-based and vegetable oil versions. Each vegan butter is slightly different in flavor and price point, but all work well for baking and sautéing.

COCONUT OIL

Pure coconut oil, not virgin, is common in many recipes because of its high fat content. Butter is typically around 65 percent saturated fat, whereas coconut oil is 90 percent saturated fat. This high fat content has its pros and cons. Coconut oil remains solid at room temperature, which makes it ideal for raw desserts like vegan cheesecake. On the other hand, though, the high fat content also makes it one of the least healthy oils.

OLIVE OIL

Olive oil is one of the most commonly used oils, and it comes with nutritious antioxidants. This oil is created by pressing olives without much other processing. Extra-virgin olive oil has the most flavor and health benefits, since it is not heat processed and comes from the first pressing of the olives. A good bottle of extra-virgin olive oil will come in a dark glass bottle or box, will taste pungent and a little bitter like fresh olives, and will have a "best by" date printed on the packaging. Rancid or poor-quality olive oil might smell like walnuts and have hints of a crayon-like flavor.

NEUTRAL OILS

Grapeseed, **peanut**, **corn**, and **vegetable oils** are the best for frying because of their high smoke points and lack of flavor. Grapeseed oil is made using a natural processing method and is high in omega-6 fatty acids, which makes it a more heart-healthy option than butter, shortening, or coconut oil. Grapeseed oil can be expensive, but its neutral flavor lets other ingredients like herbs and spices shine.

Starches and Gums

When you bake without gluten, you need starches and gums to add stability and texture to your breads, desserts, and other baked recipes; gluten-free flours like almond, sorghum, and coconut do not have the ability on their own to form cohesion, so the starches and gums lend elasticity and chew. Gums and starches each have their own specific use, based on the type of recipe and desired end product.

XANTHAN GUM

Xanthan gum is common in gluten-free products because it mimics the structure of gluten for baked goods. It is created by fermenting sugar with the bacteria *Xanthomonas campestris* and then drying and powdering the thick paste. It is widely used because it is easy to produce, allergen-free, flavorless, and odorless.

TAPIOCA STARCH

Tapioca starch is found in stores under a variety of names, such as tapioca flour and cassava flour. This common thickener can be swapped in for cornstarch with nearly identical results. The benefit of using tapioca starch over other types of starch is that it retains its thickening properties for a longer heating period. It also gives a slight sheen to sauces.

CORNSTARCH

Cornstarch is the most common thickener and the most cost friendly of the starches. However, it is high in calories and carbohydrates with little nutritional benefit.

Pasta and Grains

Pastas and grains are the foundation for many of the main dish meals because they provide volume, texture, flavor, and nutrition. The recipes in this book cover many different gluten-free grains to showcase a wide variety of unique flavors and textures.

GLUTEN-FREE PASTA

The number of available gluten-free pastas has skyrocketed in recent years. You can now get protein-rich chickpea flour, fiber-rich lentil pasta, and even low-carb konjac or shirataki noodles (Japanese noodles made from the konjac plant). The main caution when using gluten-free pastas is that they do not cook the same as wheat-based varieties, so follow the package directions carefully.

RICE

Rice is widely used as a base for meals because it is simple to cook, affordable, easy to find in any grocery store, and shelf stable. Different dishes use different types of rice based on flavor, cultural origin, or cooking time; however, types of rice can generally be swapped based on preference or availability. When choosing a type of rice, consider a few things: flavor, consistency, aroma, and nutrition. **Basmati**, a long-grain rice used in Indian dishes, is highly aromatic and low on the glycemic index (which describes how quickly your body absorbs the nutrients and, thus, how much it spikes your blood glucose levels. Lower is generally better). **Sushi rice**, a short grain, is very sticky and is the highest on the glycemic index. **Brown rice** varieties are the least processed, offer the most insoluble fiber and phytonutrients, and tend to be chewier. Recipes in this book will often call for a certain type of rice, but feel free to swap in your favorite type and adjust the cooking times as necessary.

POLENTA/GRITS

Polenta (a.k.a. grits) is made from dried and ground corn, but it is coarser than cornmeal. When cooked, polenta forms a thick porridge that is a good base for a stew, marinara sauce, or roasted veggies. When cooled, you can use it to make a cake that can be sliced and then fried, baked, or grilled.

QUINOA

Quinoa, which is actually a seed, is one of the most widely recognized health foods and can be found in any grocery store. It's so popular because it contains all nine essential amino acids, is high in protein and fiber, and has tons of vitamins and minerals. It has a slightly crunchy texture when cooked and is used often throughout this book. Be sure to rinse your quinoa before using if the package isn't labeled "pre-rinsed."

OTHER GRAINS

Gluten-free grain options have become more accessible as food businesses race to feed the growing demand. Each grain offers unique flavors and textures, and some even have a rapid cooking time. **Buckwheat groats** are nutty, large, and very chewy, which makes for a great hot breakfast cereal. **Millet** is a tiny grain with a rapid cook time and is similar in texture to couscous. **Sorghum**, a flowering grass, has pearl-like grains that make for a delightful cold grain and veggie salad. These grains are often sold in the same section as wheat grains, so it is important to check for the gluten-free label.

Other Pantry Items

A well-stocked pantry is key to ensuring that home-cooked meals happen. You don't need to have a doomsday shelter ready, but it's smart to buy some inexpensive pantry items in bulk.

BEANS

Beans, either dried or canned, offer an easy protein source for a variety of meals. The most common beans used throughout this book are **black beans**, **pinto**, **kidney**, and **cannellini**. Dried beans can be stored longer and are less processed, but they require long cooking times. Canned beans are the most convenient option but can also add a lot of sodium to recipes.

LEGUMES

Legumes are the seeds of the Fabaceae plant family and include black-eyed peas, chickpeas, peanuts, and lentils. Legumes are high in fiber and protein and are common in both gluten-free and vegan diets. Beans and legumes are often used interchangeably in recipes, but some people omit legumes from their diets because of potential inflammatory effects.

NUTS

Nuts, both raw and roasted, are common in vegan cooking because they are high in natural fats and protein. Keep a variety of them on hand, including cashews, peanuts, and walnuts, for recipes and healthy snacks. If you have a nut allergy, there are many seeds that can be used in place of nuts, like sunflower, pumpkin, and sesame seeds. Be sure to buy the raw versions of nuts and seeds if you intend to cream them.

Seasonings

Your spice cabinet is one of the most important parts of your kitchen because with the right seasonings, you can conjure just about any flavor. Also, spending a little extra on fresh, high-quality spices ensures that your dish will have the most flavor and best aroma possible.

SALT

Kosher salt is used for many of this book's recipes and will be labeled specifically. It's a larger grain, which means less salt by volume while still being plenty salty. Be careful if you swap salts, because a finer-grain salt will produce a much saltier dish. Stock your pantry with table salt, kosher salt, and flaked salt for a finishing touch to a dessert or meal.

GLUTEN-FREE TAMARI AND COCONUT AMINOS

Soy sauce contains gluten, but luckily there are two great subs: gluten-free tamari and coconut aminos. These are both delicious seasonings for soups, stews, and tofu. They both offer salty, savory, umami flavor to a variety of dishes.

NUTRITIONAL YEAST

Nutritional yeast, or as the cool vegans call it, "nooch," is an ingredient to stock up on when you dive into vegan cooking. It has a great cheesy taste, and it's used to add umami to recipes and as a topping in place of Parmesan. Plus, it's is a good source of B vitamins.

SPICES AND HERBS

Having a wide variety of flavors on hand gives you options to personalize a dish. You'll see a lot of these herbs and spices throughout the book:

- Basil

- Chili powder

- Ground coriander

- Ground cumin

- Garlic and onion powder

- Ground ginger

- Ground mustard

- Oregano

- Paprika and smoked paprika

Reading Labels

Checking product labels to ensure that they meet both vegan and gluten-free requirements can seem like a daunting task. However, there are a few tips and tricks to make grocery shopping a breeze. Buying products that are *themselves* ingredients, rather than products that *contain* ingredients, is a simple way to know exactly what you're getting. But sometimes it's nice to enjoy the convenience of prepared foods, rather than making each component of a recipe from scratch.

There are some key things to note when determining if a product is suitable for your lifestyle. All products that contain or may contain known allergens must be labeled with allergen statements. The "may contain" disclaimer is used, for example, when an otherwise gluten-free product is made or processed in the same facility as products that do contain gluten and there is a risk of cross-contamination. Products labeled "may contain gluten" are okay for those on low-gluten diets who are not allergic to gluten, but they are not safe for people who experience severe reactions to gluten.

Vegan Labeling

Animal-derived ingredients make up half of the eight major food allergens. This means that products that contain eggs, fish, shellfish, and milk must, by law, be explicitly labeled as such on food packaging.

Other non-vegan ingredients can be a little sneakier. Look out for the obvious culprits like beef, chicken, and honey. More inconspicuous non-vegan ingredients include gelatin, carmine, and L-cysteine. The term "natural flavors" can also hide a number of animal products, such as castoreum, a food additive derived from beaver glands that is often used to mimic vanilla flavor. The good news is that there are many apps available that allow you to scan a product and take away the guesswork. PETA.org, for instance, actually checks with the food companies themselves to determine if there are animal products under the vague term "natural flavors." There are also a number of vegan-certified labels that you can look out for, such as "Vegan Certified" and "Plant-Based."

Gluten-Free Labeling

Gluten is a little easier to find in an ingredient list than animal products are. As a major allergen, wheat should always be listed in the allergen statement on product packaging, even if the product only contains traces. Gluten-free products can also be easily identified by a "GF" label or "GFCO," which stands for the Gluten-Free Certification Organization.

SNEAKY NON-VEGAN FOODS

Being a vegan grocery shopper means you need to be an ingredient list super sleuth. Often a product is accidentally vegan, so isn't labeled as such, like most ketchups, Cracker Jack Caramel Coated Popcorn, and original Pringles. However, many other food products have sneaky ingredients that make them *not* vegan friendly, such as:

1. **Marshmallows:** Gelatin is the nemesis of vegans because it is in so many foods. Marshmallows almost always contain gelatin, except for vegan brands like Dandies.

2. **Granola bars:** Granola bars often sneak in non-vegan ingredients like honey and whey. Most Clif Bars and Kashi granola bars are accidentally vegan, however, and all of the LÄRABAR original fruit and nut bars and GoMacro MacroBars are vegan.

3. **Kimchi:** It is important to check the label of this delicious, spicy Korean pickle because fish paste or fish sauce is often added.

4. **Collagen:** This common beauty product and processed food additive can be produced to be vegan friendly, but, unless it is explicitly stated, collagen is primarily made with animal-based ingredients.

5. **Food coloring:** Some colors are plant-derived, but others, like Natural Red #4, is made using carmine, which comes from crushed beetles. Your best bet is to avoid all products that use food coloring or use only foods with the Certified Vegan label.

6. **Cereal:** Many popular cereals should be vegan based on the ingredients list. Yet, many fortified cereals contain vitamin D_3, which is made using sheep's lanolin.

7. **Confectioner's glaze (a.k.a. shellac):** Most candies and sprinkles use confectioner's glaze in order to get that shiny final product. Shellac is made out of crushed bugs and can also be called food glaze or natural glaze.

8. **Casein:** Casein, the main protein in dairy milk, is often hidden in the ingredient lists for products that are labeled "dairy-free." Whenever you purchase creamy soup, ice cream, sorbet, or pudding mix, look out for this sneaky additive.

9. **Salt and vinegar chips:** There are both vegan and non-vegan versions of lactic acid found in salt and vinegar chips. Whey is in the non-vegan version. Most salt and vinegar chips contain the non-vegan version, so check the label.

10. **Bread:** Whey pops up in most store-bought breads. Companies often will put "contains whey" at the end of the ingredients list.

SNEAKY SOURCES OF GLUTEN

Gluten is recognized as a major allergen, which means that gluten should be listed on product labels and ingredient lists. However, if you're allergic to gluten or experience severe reactions to gluten, pay special attention to the ingredient lists when you purchase any of these products:

1. Candy: Malt or malt extract, derived from barley (which has gluten), are commonly added to candies and chocolates as a sweetener.

2. Soy sauce: Soy sauce contains wheat and/or uses malt flavoring.

3. Beer: A variety of gluten-containing grains is used to make beer in the mash stage. There are certified gluten-free beer options.

4. Bottled salad dressing: Many salad dressings contain hidden sources of gluten, and some even have sneaky non-vegan ingredients. Malt vinegar is the main gluten-containing culprit, but also look out for Worcestershire sauce and anchovies in Caesar dressing (which are certainly not vegan).

5. Seitan and other vegan meats: Seitan, which is a popular vegan protein source, is made entirely of wheat gluten.

6. Rolled oats: Oats on their own are gluten-free; however, they often get cross-contaminated with gluten if they are grown in a field with or processed in the same facility as wheat and rye. Gluten-free oats are clearly labeled and often have a different color top than oats that may contain gluten.

7. Flavored potato chips: Malt vinegar and wheat starch are common flavor enhancers for potato chips. Soy sauce is also sometimes used to season potato chips.

8. Bouillon cubes: Bouillon cubes and other spice blends often contain maltodextrin, which can be derived from wheat. There are gluten-free options available, but it is even easier to make your own stock using leftover veggie scraps (see page 126).

9. Dried fruit: Dried fruit on its own is gluten-free, but it often gets cross-contaminated on processing equipment. If you have a gluten allergy, it is important to find dried fruit that is labeled gluten-free.

10. Soup: Cream-based or creamy options like tomato soup are often made with wheat as a thickener in the roux stage. There are gluten-free options available, and they will be clearly marked.

Essential Tools and Equipment

These essential items will make your kitchen experience easier and more fun:

1. Metal measuring spoons and cups: Spending the little bit extra for metal measuring tools is a good long-term investment because they won't warp or crack from use.

2. Baking pans: Large rimmed baking sheets (a.k.a. half sheet pans) allow you to bake and roast without the worry of your ingredients spilling over into your oven, and it's worth having more than one. A 12-mold muffin pan can be used for both muffins and cupcakes.

3. Whisks: Having at least two whisks saves you the hassle of washing one while you're in the middle of cooking. I recommend a balloon whisk, which is large and bulbous, and a narrow French whisk, which is good for smaller batches or bowls.

4. Wooden spoons and rubber spatulas: A thick wooden spoon (I like one with a little heft) is good for making stews, doughs, and sauces. You'll also need a couple of rubber spatulas of varying sizes.

5. Tongs: Tongs are either fully metal or come with high-heat silicone ends. I prefer the silicone-tipped tongs because they ensure that you won't scratch your cookware.

6. Potato masher: You'll use this tool to crush beans, break down fruits for jams and sauces, and, yes, mash potatoes.

7. Knives: A good chef's knife is an investment that will speed up your prep work and help you avoid kitchen mishaps. The sharper the knife, the less likely you are to slip while chopping slippery foods. A small santoku knife is my go-to for most chopping, but I also use my paring knife often for cutting or destemming fruit.

8. Pots and pans: It goes without saying that pots and pans are essential kitchen items, but this is truly where you should spend your kitchen money. The choice is yours between ceramic lined, nonstick, high-quality stainless steel, or cast iron. The general rule is that the heavier the pot or pan, the better it will be at heat distribution and longevity. I prefer nonstick pans because they allow me to avoid excess oil, but I also use stainless steel pots so I don't have to worry about scratching the coating when mashing or using my immersion blender. I also have a few well-seasoned cast iron pans for blackening veggies.

9. Food processor: Use this kitchen workhorse to chop veggies, break down nuts and grains, pulse cold butter into flour, and puree beans and veggies for dips.

10.Immersion blender: You can get a high-quality immersion blender for around $25, and you'll use it often for pureeing soups and making sauces.

Nice-to-Have Tools and Equipment

The more you cook, the more aware you'll become of the fun and new kitchen gadgets that can make cooking and prep easier. There are many kitchen tools that are worth the investment, but before you buy the newest and flashiest item, do a little research to see if there's other equipment that can perform a variety of tasks rather than a single task.

1. Rice cooker: A rice cooker can be used for far more than just rice. I use it to cook grains, oatmeal, risotto, and even soup without the worry of scorching or the hassle of stirring.

2. High-speed blender: A high-speed blender can have a hefty price tag, which makes it more of a want than a need. However, spending more upfront on a high-quality blender means fewer replacements and repairs later.

3. Pressure cooker: A pressure cooker can speed up cooking times and make meal prep easier.

4. Air fryer: This compact, fast-cooking tool mimics frying with little to no oil.

8 Ways to Make Gluten-Free and Vegan Work for You

If you are new to cooking without gluten and animal-based ingredients, the process might seem a bit overwhelming, but it doesn't have to be. Here are eight tips and tricks to make gluten-free and vegan cooking not just accessible but exciting and easy:

1. Cook without borders: Certain international cuisines happen to use less gluten and fewer animal-derived ingredients than others. Think Indian curries, Thai stir-fries, and Spanish paella. Travel the world without leaving the comfort of your kitchen.

2. Meal plan like a pro: Ever heard that old adage, "Failing to plan is planning to fail"? Whether it involves mapping out your meals for the week or batch cooking so you've always got a well-stocked freezer, meal planning helps reduce the stress of not knowing what to eat.

3. Shop with a list: Don't forget to write down specific brand names, especially if you share grocery duty with other people in your household; this will save confusion and reduce time spent reading labels.

4. Embrace the potluck: Food intolerances and lifestyle choices don't mean you can't get social! Potlucks are a great way to party because you know that what you're bringing is suitable for your lifestyle.

5. Become the master of packed snacks: Whether you're on a road trip or spending a long day at the office, quick, convenient snacks are crucial. Pack homemade trail mix, crispy chickpeas, roasted seaweed, and homemade granola bars.

6. Take the vitamins: If you're eating enough calories from varied sources, chances are you're getting most of the vitamins and minerals you need. However, there are some essential nutrients, such as B_{12}, that everyone should supplement—including non-vegans! If in doubt, see your doctor for a blood test to make sure your levels are A-okay. There's no shame in taking vitamins to help you feel your best.

7. Be patient: If this lifestyle is new to you, you're going to need to experiment. Not all of the foods you try are going to work out. Even if you cook something perfectly, it might not be to your taste, and you're not going to suddenly love foods you previously disliked.

8. Focus on the positives: Whether you're living the gluten-free, vegan life for health, allergy, and/or ethical reasons, focus on what you're gaining rather than on what you may be missing. Any change in lifestyle can be an adjustment, but it's also an opportunity to learn new and exciting ways to honor your body with the food that makes it feel good. You don't have to give up everything you love—you just have to think a little differently.

TROUBLESHOOTING

Cooking and baking gluten-free and vegan foods can be a whole new world for some home cooks. And it can be frustrating when you choose a great-looking recipe to try and your creation doesn't live up to the hype. Never fear; a fallen cake or off-tasting sauce happens to the best of us. This chart discusses some common problems and easy solutions.

PROBLEM	BAKED GOOD IS CRUMBLY AND DRY.	CREAM SOUP IS TOO THIN OR WATERY.	CAKES AND MUFFINS ARE TOO HEAVY.	BAKED GOOD IS FLAVORLESS.
CAUSE	Too much flour or not enough fat.	Tapioca starch was used and heated for too long, not enough starch was used, or soup lacks the needed fat.	A dense egg replacer is being used in what should be light and airy baked goods.	You reduced sugar and/or fat amounts to make it healthier.
SOLUTION	Ensure your measurements are accurate for both flour and fat.	Use a cornstarch or arrowroot starch, or thin another tablespoon of starch with water and mix it in. Or, use full-fat coconut milk or even coconut cream.	Exchange the tofu or applesauce egg replacer for a flax egg or store-bought egg replacer instead.	Use the designated amount of sugar and fat in the recipe because they are part of the ratio of baking.

SAVORY DISHES ARE UNDERWHELMING.	MEAL TASTES BLAND OR IS TOO SALTY.	PASTA, GRAINS, AND VEGETABLES ARE OVERCOOKED.	FOOD DOESN'T BROWN WHEN BAKED OR ROASTED.
Not enough spice is being used, or your spices are old.	The wrong type of salt is being used.	You boiled instead of simmered them.	The pan is overcrowded.
Check if there is a "best by" date on the spice bottle and replace as needed. Measure accurately or add more seasonings to taste.	Read the recipe carefully and use kosher salt or standard table salt as specified.	Boiling is when there are consistent active bubbles on the surface of the liquid; simmering is when bubbles come to the surface every two or three seconds. Read the recipe carefully and turn down the heat if it says to simmer.	Give your food more space on the pan or sheet so the top and sides receive heat.

Breakfast and Brunch

Chickpea Flour Omelet

ESSENTIAL RECIPE, NUT-FREE, SOY-FREE, 30 MINUTES, CROWD-PLEASER

SERVES: 2 | **PREP TIME:** 15 minutes | **COOK TIME:** 15 minutes

The combination of chickpea flour and silken tofu gives this quick recipe the texture and flavor of an omelet, perfect to fill with fresh veggies or nondairy cheese. If you can find black salt, otherwise known as kala namak, you will even have that distinct eggy flavor.

---

1 (12-ounce) container firm silken tofu

1 tablespoon tapioca starch

¼ cup chickpea flour

3 tablespoons nutritional yeast

2 tablespoons unsweetened gluten-free nondairy milk, homemade (page 218) or store-bought

1 teaspoon paprika

¼ teaspoon onion powder

¼ teaspoon ground turmeric

½ teaspoon table salt or ½ teaspoon black salt

2 tablespoons extra-virgin olive oil, divided

Up to 1 cup total filling per omelet (chopped vegetables, vegan cheese), cooked if necessary

---

1. In a blender or food processor, combine the tofu, tapioca starch, chickpea flour, nutritional yeast, milk, paprika, onion powder, turmeric, and salt; puree until smooth. Scrape the sides as needed and set aside.

2. Heat a medium nonstick pan over medium heat and add 1 tablespoon of oil. Pour half of the batter in the center of the pan and tilt the pan to spread it evenly. You can also use a dampened spatula to spread the batter.

3. Cover the pan and cook for 4 to 5 minutes or until the top doesn't jiggle when you move the pan. Place the fillings on one side of the omelet, then carefully fold the other half over to cover the filling. Cover the pan and cook for 2 minutes, then serve. Repeat to make a second omelet.

Per Serving: Calories: 500; Fat: 30g; Saturated Fat: 4g; Cholesterol: 0mg; Carbohydrates: 30g; Fiber: 12g; Protein: 34g; Sodium: 735mg

Fluffy Pancakes

ESSENTIAL RECIPE, NUT-FREE, SOY-FREE, 30 MINUTES, CROWD-PLEASER

MAKES: 8 pancakes | **PREP TIME:** 10 minutes | **COOK TIME:** 10 minutes

These light and fluffy pancakes are a weekend staple. They're more forgiving than other baked goods, making them perfect for beginners. You can substitute ¼ cup more gluten-free flour blend for the sorghum flour, or swap the vegan butter for any neutral oil, like avocado or coconut.

2 tablespoons ground flaxseed

6 tablespoons water

1 cup unsweetened gluten-free nondairy milk, homemade (page 218) or store-bought

1 teaspoon apple cider vinegar

1 cup 1:1 all-purpose gluten-free flour, homemade (page 206) or store-bought

½ cup sorghum flour

1 tablespoon baking powder

½ teaspoon baking soda

¼ teaspoon table salt

3 tablespoons vegan butter, melted, plus more as needed

1 tablespoon pure maple syrup

1. In a small bowl, whisk together the ground flaxseed and water. Set aside.

2. In another small bowl, combine the milk and vinegar. Set aside.

3. In a medium mixing bowl, whisk together the all-purpose flour, sorghum flour, baking powder, baking soda, and salt. Set aside.

4. Mix the melted butter and maple syrup into the milk mixture, then stir the milk mixture into the dry ingredients until everything is mostly combined. Add in the soaked flaxseed and mix until there are no dry spots remaining.

5. Heat a griddle or frying pan over medium-high heat. Melt a little butter to coat the surface or spray with oil. Pour ¼ cup of batter per pancake onto the griddle. Cook for 3 to 4 minutes, until the edges look dry and bubbles form in the center, then flip and finish cooking for 2 minutes.

6. Serve immediately or store in a 200°F oven to keep warm.

Per Serving (2 pancakes): Calories: 331; Fat: 11g; Saturated Fat: 2g; Cholesterol: 1mg; Carbohydrates: 52g; Fiber: 3g; Protein: 6g; Sodium: 337mg

Biscuits and Mushroom Gravy

ESSENTIAL RECIPE, NUT-FREE, SOY-FREE, 30 MINUTES, CROWD-PLEASER

SERVES: 4 | **PREP TIME:** 10 minutes, not including biscuit
prep and cook time | **COOK TIME:** 10 minutes

Biscuits and gravy are a comfort food staple typically enjoyed at breakfast, but they're great for lunch or dinner, too. The biscuits for this recipe can be found in the Basics chapter (page 187), and the gravy can be easily modified to complement other meals, such as holiday dinners.

---

3 tablespoons vegan butter, divided

8 ounces cremini mushrooms, sliced or chopped

1 small shallot, diced

1 garlic clove, minced

1 teaspoon paprika

½ teaspoon onion powder

1 tablespoon coconut aminos (see Ingredient Smarts tip)

2 tablespoons 1:1 all-purpose gluten-free flour, homemade (page 206) or store-bought

2 cups unsweetened gluten-free nondairy milk, homemade (page 218) or store-bought

Table salt

Freshly ground black pepper

8 gluten-free Drop Biscuits (page 187), warmed

Chopped scallion, green parts only, for garnish (optional)

---

1. Melt 1 tablespoon of butter in a large nonstick pan over high heat. Add the mushrooms and cook for 2 minutes without stirring. Flip the mushrooms and cook for another 2 minutes. The mushrooms should have shrunken to about half their raw size and developed slightly blackened edges. Add the shallot and garlic and sauté for 1 minute, stirring.

2. Add the paprika, onion powder, coconut aminos, and remaining 2 tablespoons of butter. Cook until the butter is melted. Sprinkle the flour on top and mix until the flour is incorporated into the butter.

3. Pour in the milk and reduce the heat to medium. Cook while gently stirring until the gravy thickens, roughly 3 to 5 minutes. Add salt and pepper to taste. Serve over warm biscuits and garnish with the scallions, if using.

CHANGE IT UP: Try serving this gravy with a variety of proteins, such as 1 cup textured vegetable protein (TVP) cooked with a gluten-free vegetarian bouillon cube, chopped and sauteed tempeh, or a premade gluten-free vegan sausage crumble. Or spoon the gravy over mashed potatoes or other cooked veggies of your choosing.

INGREDIENT SMARTS: Although its name contains the word "nut," coconut isn't a nut—it's a fruit. Most people with a nut allergy need not avoid coconut; you should, however, consult with your doctor before incorporating coconut into your diet for the first time.

Per Serving: Calories: 442; Fat: 13g; Saturated Fat: 4g; Cholesterol: 2mg; Carbohydrates: 53g; Fiber: 3g; Protein: 11g; Sodium: 570mg

Oatmeal-Pecan Waffles

ESSENTIAL RECIPE, SOY-FREE, CROWD-PLEASER

MAKES: 6 waffles | **PREP TIME:** 15 minutes | **COOK TIME:** 6 to 8 minutes per batch

Waffles are one of my favorite breakfasts because you can get really creative with flavors and add-ins, and the texture is both crispy and soft. This waffle recipe uses a combination of a gluten-free flour and gluten-free oats for a flavorful, hearty-yet-light waffle. Berries and other fruit make great additions to these waffles.

---

2 tablespoons ground golden flaxseed (see Ingredient Smarts tip)

¼ cup water

1 cup 1:1 all-purpose gluten-free flour, homemade (page 206) or store-bought

½ cup gluten-free oatmeal

2 teaspoons baking powder

½ teaspoon table salt

¼ teaspoon ground cinnamon

¾ cup unsweetened gluten-free nondairy milk, homemade (page 218) or store-bought

4 tablespoons vegan butter, melted

2 tablespoons pure maple syrup

1 teaspoon pure vanilla extract

½ cup chopped pecans

Nonstick cooking spray

---

1. In a small bowl, whisk together the flaxseed and water. Set aside.

2. In a large mixing bowl, whisk together the flour, oatmeal, baking powder, salt, and cinnamon. In a separate bowl or large measuring cup, mix together the milk, melted butter, maple syrup, and vanilla.

3. Pour the wet ingredients, including the soaked flaxseed, into the bowl with the dry ingredients and stir until no dry spots remain. Fold in the pecans and let the batter sit for 10 minutes while you heat up the waffle maker.

4. Spray the waffle maker with cooking spray. Stir the batter once or twice, then pour enough batter into the waffle maker to cover most of the cooking area. The cooking time will vary depending on your waffle maker, but most will take roughly 6 to 8 minutes.

5. Remove the cooked waffle from the iron; serve it immediately or place it on a baking sheet in a 200°F oven to keep it warm while you make the rest. Repeat with the remaining batter to make 6 waffles.

INGREDIENT SMARTS: Golden flaxseed meal is best for this recipe because it will blend in better than the more common brown flaxseed. Flaxseed meal works similarly to an egg replacer and has similar nutritional information. You can also use 2 servings of a vegan egg replacer if you don't have flaxseed meal.

Per Serving (1 waffle): Calories: 312; Fat: 16g; Saturated Fat: 2g; Cholesterol: 1mg; Carbohydrates: 36g; Fiber: 3g; Protein: 6g; Sodium: 216mg

Chickpea Flour Granola

SOY-FREE, CROWD-PLEASER, WHOLE-FOOD PLANT-BASED

MAKES: 4 cups | **PREP TIME:** 10 minutes, plus 1 hour cooling time | **COOK TIME:** 1 hour

This granola recipe is high in fiber and protein, thanks to the chickpea flour, which also lends it its crunchy, crispy texture. The batter is baked, broken into small pieces, and then mixed with dried fruit or nuts. The best part of this recipe is getting creative with the flavors, so don't be shy. Check out the Change It Up tip below, or go rogue and throw in your own favorite seasonings.

3 cups chickpea flour

¼ cup coconut sugar or brown sugar

1 teaspoon kosher salt

½ teaspoon baking powder

¼ cup pure maple syrup

2 teaspoons pure vanilla extract

¼ cup smooth almond or peanut butter

½ cup water

¼ cup unsalted sunflower seeds

½ cup hulled pumpkin seeds

1 cup unsweetened coconut flakes

1 cup mixed dried fruit (optional)

1. Preheat the oven to 350°F. Line a large rimmed baking sheet with parchment paper. Set aside.

2. In a large bowl, whisk together the chickpea flour, sugar, salt, and baking powder. Set aside. In a separate bowl, mix the maple syrup, vanilla, almond butter, and water. Mix the wet ingredients into the dry until everything is fully incorporated. Stir in the seeds and coconut flakes.

3. Scoop the mixture onto the prepared baking sheet and spread it out until it is roughly ¼ inch thick. It should cover most of the baking sheet.

4. Bake for 20 minutes. Remove the pan from the oven and use a hard spatula to cut and break the granola apart into rough 1-inch squares. It will be somewhat soft at this point, but this initial cutting will help to break it apart further in the next steps. Flip the pieces over and return the pan to the oven.

5. Bake for 10 minutes. Remove the baking sheet from the oven, use a wooden spoon to break the granola squares apart into ½-inch pieces, and then return the baking sheet to the oven. Bake in 10-minute increments, breaking the pieces down 3 more times, until the granola has cooked for a total of 1 hour. The goal is to keep breaking the pieces down with each baking segment.

6. Remove the granola from the oven. Allow it to cool on the baking sheet for 1 hour before adding dried fruit or any additional seeds and nuts. Store in an airtight container on the counter for up to 1 week or freeze in an airtight container for longer storage.

CHANGE IT UP: To spice up your granola, add a total of 1 tablespoon of spices to the batter in step 2. My favorite spice blends to add to this are apple pie spice, garam masala, Chinese five-spice powder, and even ground cinnamon and nutmeg. You can add up to ¼ cup of unsweetened cocoa powder in step 2 if you want a chocolate granola.

Per Serving (¼ cup): Calories: 170; Fat: 8g; Saturated Fat: 2g; Cholesterol: 0mg; Carbohydrates: 19g; Fiber: 3g; Protein: 6g; Sodium: 116mg

Carrot Cake Donuts

SOY-FREE, CROWD-PLEASER

MAKES: 12 donuts | **PREP TIME:** 20 minutes, plus 15 minutes
cooling time | **COOK TIME:** 18 minutes

These moist, cakey donuts derive natural sweetness from the carrots. Baking them instead of frying cuts out a lot of the mess and cook time, and that way you aren't loading up your morning with a serving of oil. Enjoy them just as they are or top them with the vegan cream cheese glaze. Don't worry if you don't have a donut pan; just make this recipe with a muffin pan instead.

FOR THE DONUTS
Nonstick cooking spray

1¾ cups 1:1 all-purpose gluten-free flour, homemade (page 206) or store-bought

1 tablespoon ground flaxseed

¼ cup vegan sugar

1 tablespoon baking powder

½ teaspoon baking soda

¼ teaspoon table salt

1 teaspoon ground cinnamon

½ cup unsweetened gluten-free nondairy milk, homemade (page 218) or store-bought

1 cup no-added-sugar applesauce

1 teaspoon pure vanilla extract

1 cup finely shredded carrot (roughly 1 large carrot)

¼ cup chopped walnuts

FOR THE CREAM CHEESE GLAZE (OPTIONAL)
3 tablespoons vegan cream cheese, at room temperature

¼ cup powdered sugar

1 teaspoon pure vanilla extract

2 to 3 tablespoons unsweetened gluten-free nondairy milk, homemade (page 218) or store-bought

1. Place a rack in the middle of the oven and preheat to 375°F. Lightly spray 2 donut pans with cooking spray. Set aside.

2. To make the donuts: In a large mixing bowl, whisk together the flour, ground flaxseed, sugar, baking powder, baking soda, salt, and cinnamon. In a small mixing bowl, combine the milk, applesauce, and vanilla.

3. Mix the wet ingredients into the dry ingredients until no dry clumps remain.

4. Fold the carrots and walnuts into the mix until fully incorporated.

5. Fill each donut mold to just below the top with the batter, approximately 3 to 4 tablespoons per donut.

6. Place both pans in the oven on the middle rack and bake for 16 to 18 minutes. Remove from the oven and let the donuts rest in the pan for 2 minutes. Carefully remove the donuts from the pan, one at a time, and place them on a wire rack to cool before serving or glazing. Giving them time to cool on the wire rack lets moisture evaporate; they will firm up before serving.

7. To make the cream cheese glaze: In a small bowl, use a fork to mix together the cream cheese, sugar, and vanilla. Start with 2 tablespoons of milk and add more as necessary. Spoon the glaze over the cooled donuts.

Per Serving (1 donut): Calories: 138; Fat: 2g; Saturated Fat: 0g; Cholesterol: 0mg; Carbohydrates: 28g; Fiber: 2g; Protein: 2g; Sodium: 114mg

Spiced Almond Butter Quesadillas

SOY-FREE, 30 MINUTES, CROWD-PLEASER

SERVES: 2 | **PREP TIME:** 5 minutes, not including salsa preparation | **COOK TIME:** 6 minutes

This simple yet flavorful breakfast is a quick way to break out of the oatmeal blues. You can also top the quesadillas with additional fresh fruit, toasted coconut, or a mix of your favorite seeds.

¼ cup smooth almond butter

1 tablespoon fresh orange zest (from about ½ orange)

2 tablespoons pure maple syrup

½ teaspoon kosher salt

1 teaspoon ground ginger

1 teaspoon ground cinnamon

1 teaspoon pure vanilla extract

8 small corn tortillas

1 tablespoon avocado oil, divided

½ cup Fresh Berry and Mint Salsa (page 215)

---

1. In a medium bowl, combine the almond butter, orange zest, maple syrup, salt, ginger, cinnamon, and vanilla.

2. Evenly divide the spiced almond butter mixture over 4 tortillas and then place a tortilla on the top of each.

3. In a large nonstick frying pan, heat ½ tablespoon of oil over medium-high heat and spread it evenly over the surface. Place the prepared tortillas into the pan and cook for 3 minutes. Remove from the pan and place on a wire rack or plate. Add the remaining ½ tablespoon of oil to the pan, spread to coat the surface, and cook the other side of the tortillas for 3 minutes.

4. Serve warm, topped with the salsa and any desired toppings.

CHANGE IT UP: You can substitute lemon or lime zest for the orange, but don't cut zest entirely; it adds a brightness to the almond butter that complements the berry salsa.

Per Serving: Calories: 568; Fat: 27g; Saturated Fat: 3g; Cholesterol: 0mg; Carbohydrates: 75g; Fiber: 10g; Protein: 13g; Sodium: 599mg

Very Berry Vanilla Smoothie

SOY-FREE, 30 MINUTES, CROWD-PLEASER, WHOLE-FOOD PLANT-BASED

SERVES: 2 | **PREP TIME:** 5 minutes

A smoothie is a delicious way to start your day by loading up on nutrients like vitamins and minerals, fiber, and protein. I like to use a combination of fresh banana and frozen cauliflower florets (don't worry, they add no flavor) as my creamy, healthy base, then add in other fresh or frozen items. Customize this recipe in any way you like.

---

2 large ripe bananas

1 cup frozen cauliflower florets

1 cup frozen raspberries

1 cup frozen blueberries

1 cup frozen strawberries

2 tablespoons almond or cashew butter

1 tablespoon pure vanilla extract

1 tablespoon chia seeds

2 cups unsweetened gluten-free nondairy milk, homemade (page 218) or store-bought

Water, for thinning (optional)

In a blender, combine the bananas, cauliflower, raspberries, blueberries, strawberries, almond butter, vanilla, chia seeds, and milk. Blend until creamy, scrape the sides as needed, and add a cup of water or more milk to reach your desired thickness. Serve immediately.

INGREDIENT SMARTS: I like using frozen fruit and fresh bananas to get a cold and creamy consistency without adding ice, which can make the smoothie watery. If you want even more protein, add some unsweetened pea protein. Most brands of pea protein, like Bob's Red Mill, offer over 20 grams of protein per serving.

Per Serving: Calories: 489; Fat: 13g; Saturated Fat: 2g; Cholesterol: 5mg; Carbohydrates: 81g; Fiber: 18g; Protein: 17g; Sodium: 187mg

Sweet Potato Waffled Tofu

NUT-FREE, 30 MINUTES, CROWD-PLEASER, WHOLE-FOOD PLANT-BASED

MAKES: 2 waffles | **PREP TIME:** 15 minutes | **COOK TIME:** 20 minutes

A waffle maker is perfect for crisping root veggies like sweet potato. You can omit the curry powder or substitute it with another seasoning blend of your choosing, like vindaloo, berbere, Old Bay, or a lemon pepper mix.

---

1 (14-ounce) package firm tofu

2 tablespoons ground flaxseed

4 tablespoons water

1 large sweet potato, peeled

1 small yellow onion, diced

2 tablespoons minced scallion, white part only

1 tablespoon pure maple syrup

1 tablespoon curry powder

1 teaspoon kosher salt

Nonstick cooking spray

---

1. Cut the tofu block in half widthwise so that each piece is roughly ½ inch thick. Place the tofu on a paper towel–lined cutting board that is propped up on one end and angled slightly to drain any excess moisture into your sink or a pan.

2. In a small bowl, mix together the ground flaxseed and water, and set aside.

3. Into a medium mixing bowl, shred the sweet potato. Mix in the soaked flaxseed, the onion and scallion, maple syrup, curry powder, and salt.

4. Heat your waffle maker and spray the top and bottom surfaces with a liberal amount of cooking spray. Spoon one-quarter of the mixture onto the center of the bottom cooking surface. Spread it out to be the same size as the tofu piece. Place a piece of tofu on top and then spoon out one-quarter more of the mixture to top the tofu and spread to cover.

5. Slowly press the top of the waffle maker down until it closes and latches. Cook for 10 minutes. Remove the waffle and place it on a wire rack to cool for 5 minutes before serving. You can also place the waffle on a baking sheet in a 200°F oven to stay warm until the second waffle is finished. Repeat for the second waffle. Enjoy as is, or serve with a sprinkle of curry powder, chopped scallion tops, sriracha, or maple syrup.

Per Serving (1 waffle): Calories: 465; Fat: 23g; Saturated Fat: 3g; Cholesterol: 0mg; Carbohydrates: 37g; Fiber: 11g; Protein: 38g; Sodium: 888mg

Sweet Potato Hash with Adobo

NUT-FREE, SOY-FREE, CROWD-PLEASER, WHOLE-FOOD PLANT-BASED

SERVES: 2 | **PREP TIME:** 10 minutes | **COOK TIME:** 35 minutes

I like to keep a few easy, savory brunch dishes on the roster. This recipe gets flavor inspiration from the Southwest by pairing the earthy spice of adobo with the natural sweetness of corn and scallion.

---

1 large sweet potato, peeled and cut into ¼-inch cubes

1 medium yellow onion, diced

2 garlic cloves, minced

¼ cup nutritional yeast

1 teaspoon kosher salt

1 tablespoon ground cumin

1 tablespoon smoked paprika

¼ cup water, plus more as needed

1 tablespoon adobo sauce (see Ingredient Smarts tip below)

1 (15-ounce) can black beans, drained and rinsed

1 (15-ounce) can corn, drained, or 1½ cups frozen

¼ cup roughly chopped scallion tops (green part only)

½ cup Sunflower Seed Cheese Sauce (page 210) (optional, but it's really good!)

---

1. In a large nonstick frying pan over high heat, cook the sweet potato and onion for 5 minutes, stirring. Add 1 tablespoon of water as needed to avoid cooking the onion too quickly. Reduce the heat to medium and cook undisturbed for 10 minutes.

2. Stir in the garlic, nutritional yeast, salt, cumin, and paprika. Pour the water over the top, stir, and cook for 5 minutes.

3. Drizzle the adobo sauce over the mixture and stir in the black beans and corn. Cook for 5 minutes, stirring occasionally.

4. Serve with the scallions and cheese sauce, if desired.

Per Serving: Calories: 397; Fat: 4g; Saturated Fat: 1g; Cholesterol: 0mg; Carbohydrates: 76g; Fiber: 20g; Protein: 22g; Sodium: 932mg

Scrambled Tofu–Stuffed Breakfast Peppers

ESSENTIAL RECIPE, NUT-FREE, CROWD-PLEASER, WHOLE-FOOD PLANT-BASED

SERVES: 4 | **PREP TIME:** 20 minutes | **COOK TIME:** 50 minutes

These cheesy breakfast peppers are a great savory breakfast option that can be prepared ahead for an easy morning meal. If you want to save even more time, skip baking the scramble in the peppers and enjoy delicious scrambled tofu with a side of crusty gluten-free toast and avocado. No matter how you make it, the protein and fiber will keep you satisfied throughout your morning.

---

2 tablespoons nutritional yeast

1 tablespoon yellow miso

2 teaspoons paprika

½ teaspoon garlic powder

1 teaspoon onion powder

1 teaspoon liquid smoke

½ cup water

1 (14-ounce) package firm tofu

1 medium carrot, diced

4 medium bell peppers

Salsa, for serving (optional)

Sunflower Seed Cheese Sauce (page 210, optional), for serving

---

1. In a small measuring cup, mix together the nutritional yeast, miso, paprika, garlic powder, onion powder, liquid smoke, and water. Set aside.

2. Heat a large nonstick frying pan over high heat. Using your hands, crumble the tofu into the frying pan so that it is mostly ½-inch pieces. Cook undisturbed for 5 minutes. Reduce the heat to medium, add the carrot, and cook, stirring occasionally, for 10 minutes, until the carrot can be easily pierced by a fork.

3. Pour the nutritional yeast mixture over the tofu scramble, gently mix, and cook for 5 minutes, until the liquid is gone. You can serve it at this stage (I like it topped with chopped scallions) or continue to stuff the peppers.

4. Preheat the oven to 350°F. Cut the tops off of the bell peppers and discard the core. If necessary, cut a small slice off the bottom so they stand upright. Divide the scrambled tofu among the four peppers and place them in an 8-by-8-inch glass baking dish so they are standing upright.

5. Add just enough water to the bottom of the dish to cover the surface, less than ¼ cup, cover the dish with aluminum foil, and bake for 20 minutes. Remove the foil and bake for an additional 10 minutes.

6. Serve warm, topped with salsa or cheese sauce, if using.

MAKE AHEAD: Stuffed peppers are a great make-ahead meal. Just assemble them through step 4 (without preheating the oven), cover the pan with foil, and refrigerate. When you're ready to bake the peppers, preheat the oven and proceed with step 5.

CHANGE IT UP: This recipe stuffs the peppers with carrots and tofu, but you could also add in or use premade lentils, quinoa and beans, or refried beans with veggies and Enchilada Sauce (page 214).

Per Serving: Calories: 210; Fat: 10g; Saturated Fat: 1g; Cholesterol: 0mg; Carbohydrates: 16g; Fiber: 6g; Protein: 19g; Sodium: 322mg

Strawberry Breakfast Bruschetta

NUT-FREE, SOY-FREE, 30 MINUTES, CROWD-PLEASER,
WHOLE-FOOD PLANT-BASED

SERVES: 4 | **PREP TIME:** 20 minutes

This sweet, fresh bruschetta is a great, quick breakfast option. Here, I've combined basil, which is in the mint family, with sweet-tart strawberries and aromatic lemon zest. It is delicious served on Seeded Sandwich Bread (page 200), and don't forget to drizzle it with the caramel for even more flavor.

- 2 cups chopped fresh strawberries
- 1 tablespoon lemon zest (from about ½ lemon)
- 1 teaspoon chopped fresh basil
- ¼ teaspoon table salt
- ¼ teaspoon freshly ground black pepper, plus more for topping
- 4 slices bread (such as Seeded Sandwich Bread, page 200), toasted
- 2 cups fresh arugula or watercress
- 2 tablespoons Date Caramel Sauce (page 213) or agave syrup

---

1. In a medium mixing bowl, combine the strawberries, lemon zest, basil, salt, and pepper. Use a wooden spoon to mix the ingredients and lightly mash the strawberries.

2. Cut each slice of toast in half so there are 8 thin strips of toast.

3. Divide the arugula among the toast strips, then top each piece of toast with some of the strawberry mixture. Drizzle a little Date Caramel Sauce or agave syrup on each slice and top with freshly ground black pepper.

CHANGE IT UP: Instead of the strawberry mixture, spread a dollop of almond ricotta or vegan cream cheese on the toast, then top with the arugula. Or, you can skip the greens entirely (especially if you're making this for kids).

Per Serving: Calories: 262; Fat: 10g; Saturated Fat: 1g; Cholesterol: 1mg; Carbohydrates: 46g; Fiber: 5g; Protein: 6g; Sodium: 310mg

Jicama Hash Browns

NUT-FREE, SOY-FREE, 30 MINUTES, CROWD-PLEASER

SERVES: 4 | **PREP TIME:** 15 minutes | **COOK TIME:** 15 minutes

Jicama is a mild, crunchy, nutrient-dense root vegetable native to Mexico. It has gained popularity recently as a superfood, thanks to its high levels of gut-friendly fiber and vitamin C. Don't be fooled by its potato-y looks; jicama is sweet and crispy, and it gives an entirely new spin to classic hash browns. These patties are delicious topped with mashed avocado for a stand-alone breakfast.

1 large jicama, peeled and shredded

½ teaspoon table salt

1 small yellow onion, thinly sliced

½ teaspoon garlic powder

1 teaspoon smoked paprika

2 tablespoons avocado oil

1. Place the shredded jicama in a large colander, sprinkle with the salt, and let it drain over a bowl or in the sink for 5 minutes.

2. Squeeze the jicama to release any excess liquid, then put the jicama in a large bowl. Add the onion, garlic powder, and paprika and mix until everything is evenly incorporated. Divide the mixture into four equal portions; use your hands to form each portion into a ball.

3. In a skillet, heat the oil over medium heat. Place the jicama patties in the pan, then flatten them with a spatula. Cook on one side for 10 minutes, flip the patties, and cook for 5 more minutes or until nicely browned on both sides.

Per Serving: Calories: 186; Fat: 7g; Saturated Fat: 1g; Cholesterol: 0mg; Carbohydrates: 29g; Fiber: 15g; Protein: 3g; Sodium: 304mg

Cinnamon Rolls

NUT-FREE, SOY-FREE, CROWD-PLEASER

MAKES: 12 rolls | **PREP TIME:** 30 minutes, plus 4 hours for
rising and resting | **COOK TIME:** 25 minutes

Classic cinnamon rolls shouldn't just be for special occasions or lazy weekends. These cinnamon rolls can be prepped ahead and stored in the freezer or refrigerator until you're ready to bake them. This gluten-free version uses soaked flaxseed meal to give stability to the dough, and the rising time gives the rolls added flavor and color.

FOR THE DOUGH

2 tablespoons ground flaxseed

¼ cup water

½ cup vegan sugar

4½ cups 1:1 all-purpose gluten-free flour, homemade (page 206) or store-bought

1½ tablespoons instant dry yeast

½ teaspoon table salt

1¼ cup unsweetened gluten-free nondairy milk, homemade (page 218) or store-bought

½ cup melted vegan butter

FOR THE FILLING

6 tablespoons vegan butter, at room temperature

½ cup vegan light brown sugar

2 tablespoons ground cinnamon

FOR THE GLAZE

2 cups vegan powdered sugar

2 tablespoons melted vegan butter

2 teaspoons pure vanilla extract

3 to 4 tablespoons unsweetened gluten-free nondairy milk, homemade (page 218) or store-bought

1. To make the dough: In a small bowl, whisk together the ground flaxseed and water. Set aside.

2. In a large mixing bowl, whisk together the sugar, flour, instant yeast, and salt.

3. Pour in the milk, melted butter, and soaked flaxseed. Mix together with a heavy spoon. Once all the dry ingredients have been incorporated, pour the dough onto a lightly floured counter and knead for 2 to 5 minutes or until the dough is smooth. Place the dough in a lightly oiled bowl, cover it with a lid or plastic wrap, and let it rise at room temperature for 2 hours.

4. To make the filling: In a small bowl, mix together the butter, brown sugar, and cinnamon. Set aside.

5. Place the dough ball on a clean, unfloured work surface, and roll it out until it's roughly ½ inch thick, about a 12-by-18-inch rectangle. Spread the filling out evenly over the dough, leaving a ½-inch gap on one of the long ends.

6. Roll the dough up, moving toward the gap, pulling back gently to form a tighter roll. Let the dough sit, seam-side down, while you oil the inside of a 9-by-13-inch glass baking dish.

7. Using a sharp knife, cut the roll into 12 pieces. Use a light sawing action to avoid compressing the rolls. Place the rolls in the prepared baking dish. Cover the dish with plastic wrap. Refrigerate overnight or let the rolls sit on the countertop for 2 hours before proceeding to baking.

8. If the rolls were refrigerated, let them warm to room temperature for 1 hour while you preheat the oven to 375°F.

9. Remove the plastic wrap from the baking dish. Bake the rolls for 20 to 25 minutes, until the tops of the rolls are lightly browned. Remove the rolls from the oven, and place the baking pan on a wire rack to cool.

10. To make the glaze: Whisk together the powdered sugar, butter, vanilla, and milk while your cinnamon rolls are cooling. Add more milk if you prefer a runnier consistency. Drizzle over the rolls before serving.

Per Serving (1 roll): Calories: 493; Fat: 17g; Saturated Fat: 3g; Cholesterol: 1mg; Carbohydrates: 81g; Fiber: 3g; Protein: 5g; Sodium: 120mg

Triple Berry Toasty Tarts

NUT-FREE, SOY-FREE, CROWD-PLEASER

MAKES: 16 pastries | **PREP TIME:** 2 hours | **COOK TIME:** 45 minutes

My version of the iconic tasty toaster treat is made using an easy shortbread cookie dough that is rolled thin, filled with a simple homemade triple berry jam, and baked. Cut it into individual servings and serve warm, or as a special breakfast the next day.

FOR THE TRIPLE BERRY JAM

1 cup blueberries, fresh or frozen

1 cup raspberries, fresh or frozen

1 cup hulled strawberries, fresh or frozen

3 tablespoons pure maple syrup

1 tablespoon freshly squeezed lemon juice

½ cup water

3 tablespoons cornstarch

FOR THE DOUGH

2 cups 1:1 all-purpose gluten-free flour, homemade (page 206) or store-bought

1 tablespoon vegan sugar

½ teaspoon table salt

¾ cup chilled unsalted vegan butter, cut into ½-tablespoon pieces

4 to 5 tablespoons ice water

FOR THE GLAZE

1½ cups vegan powdered sugar

1 teaspoon ground cinnamon

2 tablespoons unsweetened gluten-free nondairy milk, homemade (page 218) or store-bought

1 teaspoon pure vanilla extract

1. To make the triple berry jam: In a medium pot over medium heat, combine the blueberries, raspberries, and strawberries and cook until they have thawed (if frozen) and can be mashed using a heavy spoon. Stir in the maple syrup and lemon juice and cook for 5 minutes. In a small bowl, mix together the water and cornstarch. Pour the cornstarch mixture into the pot with the berries, stir, and heat until the jam thickens, about 1 minute. Remove from the heat and let cool while you make the dough.

2. To make the dough: In a food processor, combine the flour, sugar, and salt; pulse 3 or 4 times to mix. If you don't have a food processor, whisk these ingredients together in a bowl.

3. Add the cold butter pieces to the flour mixture, and pulse 3 or 4 times to break up the butter into pea-size pieces. Alternatively, you can use a pastry cutter or 2 forks to cut the butter into the flour mixture.

4. Add 1 tablespoon of cold water at a time. Pulse 2 or 3 times (or mix with a spoon), then add the next tablespoon of water. Stop adding water and pulsing when the mixture sticks together when you squeeze it.

5. Turn the dough onto a clean, unfloured work surface. Press the dough into a ball, then flatten it into a 1-inch-thick disk. Wrap the dough disk in plastic wrap and refrigerate for 30 minutes to 1 hour.

6. Preheat the oven to 350°F.

7. Divide the dough in half. Place one half on a sheet of parchment paper on your work surface; rewrap the other half in plastic wrap and refrigerate. Press the dough into a rectangle, top with another sheet of parchment, and roll out the dough to ¼-inch to ⅛-inch thickness. Remove the top layer of parchment, and transfer the rolled dough and bottom sheet of parchment to a large rimmed baking sheet. Roll out the remaining piece of dough in the same way; set aside.

8. Spread the jam on the first dough rectangle, leaving a ½-inch edge. Place the second sheet of dough on top, and crimp and seal the edges with a fork.

9. Bake for 35 to 45 minutes, until the top of the pastry is lightly browned. Remove the baking sheet from the oven, and let the pastry cool for 30 minutes to 1 hour before topping with the glaze.

10. To make the glaze: Whisk together the powdered sugar, cinnamon, milk, and vanilla in a small bowl. Add more milk as needed to reach your desired consistency. Drizzle the glaze over the pastry, smoothing it with an offset spatula or the back of a spoon. Slice and serve, or store in an airtight container at room temperature for up to 1 week.

Per Serving (1 pastry): Calories: 216; Fat: 9g; Saturated Fat: 2g; Cholesterol: 0mg; Carbohydrates: 33g; Fiber: 2g; Protein: 1g; Sodium: 77mg

CHAPTER 3

Appetizers, Snacks, and Beverages

< Plantain Chips with Lime
Yogurt Sauce, page **60**, and
Pineapple-Turmeric-
Ginger Lemonade, page **62**

Cheesecake Dip

SOY-FREE, 30 MINUTES, CROWD-PLEASER, WHOLE-FOOD PLANT-BASED

SERVES: 4 | **PREP TIME:** 15 minutes

This sweet dip is perfect for serving with gluten-free shortbread cookies, apple slices, or on celery with raisins for an "ants-on-a-log" snack. Even though the name implies a decadent, sugary treat, this dip is made primarily with chickpeas and is sweetened with dates and maple syrup. Not only is it healthy, but it also comes together in just a few minutes. In the recipe instructions, you'll see a peeling method for the chickpeas. This method ensures a smooth consistency that is similar to that of cookie dough.

---

6 pitted Medjool dates

¼ cup boiling water

1 (15-ounce) can chickpeas, drained and rinsed

1 tablespoon freshly squeezed lemon juice

¼ teaspoon kosher salt

¼ cup white rice flour

1 teaspoon pure vanilla extract

2 tablespoons pure maple syrup

---

1. In a measuring cup, combine the dates and boiling water; let sit for 15 minutes while you prepare the other ingredients.

2. Remove the skins of the chickpeas to make your dip even smoother. You can remove the skins by pinching the chickpea between your thumb and index finger so that the chickpea pops through the skin. Alternatively, you can pour the drained chickpeas into a bowl, fill the bowl with water, rub the chickpeas between your hands so the skins come off, then pour the water slowly out so that the floating skins leave the bowl and the chickpeas stay at the bottom.

3. In a food processor or high-speed blender, combine the dates and their water, the chickpeas, lemon juice, salt, rice flour, vanilla, and maple syrup and process until smooth. Scrape the sides down as needed. Add more water, 1 tablespoon at a time, if you want a smoother consistency.

4. This can be served immediately, but it is even better when it is chilled for 1 hour or up to overnight.

Per Serving: Calories: 244; Fat: 2g; Saturated Fat: 0g; Cholesterol: 0mg; Carbohydrates: 55g; Fiber: 6g; Protein: 5g; Sodium: 239mg

Tahini and Seeds Granola Bars

NUT-FREE, SOY-FREE, CROWD-PLEASER, WHOLE-FOOD PLANT-BASED

MAKES: 16 bars | **PREP TIME:** 10 minutes, plus 30 minutes cooling time | **COOK TIME:** 5 minutes

It is nearly impossible to find a granola bar at the store that is both vegan and gluten-free, and the ones that are typically consist primarily of pureed dates. Thanks to a little bit of candy-making science, these granola bars are both chewy and crunchy, and they are made with all-natural ingredients.

Nonstick cooking spray

2 cups gluten-free oats

¼ cup sunflower seeds

¼ cup sesame seeds

¼ cup unsweetened coconut flakes

1 cup pure maple syrup

½ cup tahini

1 teaspoon pure vanilla extract

1. Coat an 8-by-8-inch baking dish lightly with cooking spray. In a large bowl, mix together the oats, sunflower seeds, sesame seeds, and coconut flakes. Set aside.

2. In a small saucepan, cook the maple syrup over medium-high heat, stirring continuously, until the entire surface is bubbling. Turn the heat to low and cook for exactly 5 minutes, continuing to stir. Turn off the heat and stir in the tahini and vanilla until the mixture is smooth.

3. Pour the maple syrup–tahini mixture into the oat mixture, and stir until all the oats are covered. Press the mixture into the prepared baking dish. Allow to sit at room temperature for 30 minutes, then cut into 16 servings. Wrap the bars in plastic wrap; store them at room temperature for up to 1 week.

TECHNIQUE TIP: If the heat is too high when you cook the maple syrup, you might cause the syrup to burn. Make sure to follow the instructions; turn the heat to low once bubbles form on the surface of the heated syrup and cook for only as long as stated.

Per Serving (1 bar): Calories: 193; Fat: 5g; Saturated Fat: 1g; Cholesterol: 0mg; Carbohydrates: 27g; Fiber: 3g; Protein: 8g; Sodium: 13mg

Tofu Nuggets

NUT-FREE, CROWD-PLEASER, WHOLE-FOOD PLANT-BASED

SERVES: 8 | **PREP TIME:** 20 minutes | **COOK TIME:** 45 minutes

These tofu nuggets can be baked and frozen for future meals. Not only will they become a quick favorite, but they'll also give you an excuse to test out every sauce in the Basics chapter, like the Buffalo Sauce (page 221).

---

2 (14-ounce) packages firm or extra-firm tofu

1½ cups 1:1 all-purpose gluten-free flour, homemade (page 206) or store-bought

½ cup cornstarch

½ cup gluten-free panko breadcrumbs

1 teaspoon baking powder

1 teaspoon table salt

½ teaspoon onion powder

½ teaspoon garlic powder

1 teaspoon paprika

2½ cups unsweetened gluten-free nondairy milk, homemade (page 218) or store-bought

1 tablespoon avocado oil

Nonstick cooking spray

---

1. Preheat the oven to 350°F. Line a rimmed baking sheet with parchment.

2. Cut each block of tofu into nugget-size (1-by-2-inch) pieces and place on the prepared baking sheet. Bake for 20 minutes (this step improves the texture of the final product). Remove the tofu from the oven, but keep the oven on. Allow the tofu to cool on the pan.

3. In a food processor or blender, combine the flour, cornstarch, breadcrumbs, baking powder, salt, onion powder, garlic powder, paprika, milk, and oil; puree until smooth. Pour the batter into a shallow bowl.

4. Dip each piece of tofu into the batter, then place on the baking sheet.

5. Bake for 15 minutes. Spray the tops with cooking spray, flip, spray the other side, and bake for 10 more minutes, until the nuggets look slightly golden and the coating is firm to the touch.

Per Serving: Calories: 273; Fat: 9g; Saturated Fat: 1g; Cholesterol: 0mg; Carbohydrates: 36g; Fiber: 2g; Protein: 15g; Sodium: 343mg

Spiced Pecans

SOY-FREE, CROWD-PLEASER

SERVES: 8 | **PREP TIME:** 10 minutes, plus 15 minutes
cooling time | **COOK TIME:** 10 minutes

These spiced pecans are highly aromatic with a little lingering heat. If you're looking for something to bring to a get-together or take with you for a snack, these nuts perfectly fit the bill.

1 teaspoon kosher salt

1 teaspoon Chinese five-spice powder

¼ teaspoon ground white pepper

1 pound unsalted pecans

4 tablespoons unsalted vegan butter, cut into tablespoon-size slices

1 teaspoon orange zest

¼ cup pure maple syrup

2 tablespoons water

1. Line a large rimmed baking sheet with parchment paper. Set aside.

2. In a small bowl, mix the salt, five-spice powder, and pepper. Set aside.

3. Heat a medium cast iron skillet or nonstick frying pan over medium heat. Spread the pecans across the pan in a single layer. Cook, stirring frequently, for 5 minutes or until the nuts are lightly browned on all sides.

4. Add the butter and stir until it melts. Stir in the orange zest, then sprinkle the spice mixture over top and stir for 1 minute. Pour the maple syrup and water over the nuts and cook, stirring, until the nuts are evenly coated and there's no visible liquid in the pan, about 3 minutes.

5. Transfer the nuts to the prepared baking sheet and separate them so they cool more evenly. Allow the nuts to cool completely, about 15 minutes, then transfer them to an airtight container for storage. They can be stored on the countertop for up to 3 weeks or frozen for longer storage.

Per Serving: Calories: 468; Fat: 47g; Saturated Fat: 5g; Cholesterol: 0mg; Carbohydrates: 15g; Fiber: 5g; Protein: 5g; Sodium: 207mg

Smoky Tempeh-Stuffed Mushrooms

NUT-FREE

MAKES: 16 stuffed mushrooms | **PREP TIME:** 30 minutes | **COOK TIME:** 30 minutes

Stuffed mushrooms are a must-have in your appetizer arsenal. These are loaded with smoky tempeh and sun-dried tomatoes, then topped with crispy bread-crumbs. The combination of the umami from the mushrooms and the smoke in the tempeh is eye-closing good.

16 cremini mushrooms

1 (8-ounce) package tempeh

1 tablespoon smoked paprika

1 teaspoon onion powder

1 teaspoon garlic powder

1 teaspoon liquid smoke

1 small yellow onion, diced

1 tablespoon coconut aminos

¼ cup sun-dried tomatoes, chopped (see Ingredient Smarts tip)

½ cup gluten-free panko breadcrumbs

1 tablespoon Italian seasoning

1 tablespoon extra-virgin olive oil

1. Preheat the oven to 350°F. Line a large rimmed baking sheet with parchment paper.

2. Use a spoon to remove the stem and some of the center from the mushrooms. Set the stems aside.

3. Finely dice the tempeh and mushroom stems. Heat a large nonstick frying pan over medium-high heat, and cook the tempeh and mushroom stems, stirring, for 5 minutes. Add the paprika, onion powder, garlic powder, liquid smoke, and onion. Stir to combine, and cook for 5 additional minutes, until the onions are translucent and any liquid in the pan has evaporated. Mix in the coconut aminos and sun-dried tomatoes. Remove the pan from the heat and set aside.

4. In a small bowl, mix together the panko, Italian seasoning, and oil.

5. Press roughly 1 tablespoon of tempeh filling into each mushroom cap, then lightly press a teaspoon of the panko topping on each. Place them on the prepared baking sheet.

6. Bake for 20 to 25 minutes or until the panko starts to brown. Serve immediately.

INGREDIENT SMARTS: The sun-dried tomatoes for this recipe should be moist and soft. If your sun-dried tomatoes are hard, they should be soaked in warm water before using.

Per Serving (2 mushrooms): Calories: 107; Fat: 5g; Saturated Fat: 1g; Cholesterol: 0mg; Carbohydrates: 9g; Fiber: 1g; Protein: 8g; Sodium: 119mg

Candied Coconut Cashews

SOY-FREE, CROWD-PLEASER

MAKES: 2½ cups | **PREP TIME:** 5 minutes | **COOK TIME:** 1 hour

These coconut cashews are simple to make and only take about 5 minutes to prep before baking. The lime-infused syrup and flaked coconut in this recipe make for a crispy, flavorful snack. They're also a great gift for the coconut lover in your life.

½ cup vegan sugar

½ cup unsweetened desiccated coconut

1 tablespoon lime zest

½ teaspoon table salt

¼ cup aquafaba (the liquid from canned chickpeas; see Ingredient Smarts tip)

½ teaspoon cream of tartar

2 cups roasted unsalted cashews

1 teaspoon pure vanilla extract

---

1. Preheat the oven to 275°F. Line a large rimmed baking sheet with parchment paper. Set aside.

2. In a large bowl, mix together the sugar, coconut, lime zest, and salt.

3. In a large measuring cup or small bowl, whisk together the aquafaba and cream of tartar until frothy with a soft peak.

4. Add the cashews and vanilla to the aquafaba mixture and mix until the nuts are completely coated.

5. Pour the nuts into the bowl with the coconut and sugar; mix and toss or stir until the nuts are completely coated. Dump the mixture onto the prepared baking sheet, and spread out the coated cashews in a single layer with minimal touching.

6. Bake for 1 hour, flipping the cashews once or twice and turning the pan each time you stir to avoid oven hot spots. Remove the baking sheet from the oven, set it on a wire rack, and allow the nuts to cool completely. Store in an airtight container on the countertop for up to 3 weeks or in the freezer for longer storage.

INGREDIENT SMARTS: Aquafaba, the thick liquid from canned chickpeas, is infused with fiber and protein from the canning process, and it can be whipped to a soft peak stage using just a little cream of tartar. Aquafaba is a good oil substitute in recipes like this because it works to both crisp the nuts and bind the spices and other ingredients without making the nuts too wet.

Per Serving (¼ cup): Calories: 212; Fat: 14g; Saturated Fat: 4g; Cholesterol: 0mg; Carbohydrates: 18g; Fiber: 1g; Protein: 4g; Sodium: 122mg

Panko Jalapeño Poppers

NUT-FREE, SOY-FREE, CROWD-PLEASER

MAKES: 24 jalapeño poppers | **PREP TIME:** 20 minutes, plus
5 minutes cooling | **COOK TIME:** 22 minutes

Fresh jalapeño peppers are stuffed with cheesy mashed chickpeas, onion, and spices, then breaded in gluten-free panko and baked until golden and bubbly. They're the perfect game day snack!

---

12 jalapeño peppers

1 (15-ounce) can chickpeas, drained and rinsed

1 teaspoon garlic powder

1 cup vegan shredded cheddar cheese

2 tablespoons finely chopped chives

¼ cup gluten-free panko breadcrumbs

1 tablespoon vegan butter, melted

---

1. Preheat the oven to 400°F. Line a large rimmed baking sheet with parchment paper.

2. Slice the jalapeños in half lengthwise and use a spoon to scoop out the seeds and the white pith.

3. In a large bowl, mash the chickpeas using a potato masher or heavy wooden spoon. Mix in the garlic powder, cheese, and chives. In a separate bowl, combine the panko crumbs and melted butter.

4. Fill the jalapeños with the chickpea and cheese mixture. Top each with the panko mix.

5. Place the loaded jalapeños on the prepared baking sheet and bake for 20 to 22 minutes, until the tops are golden brown.

6. Cool on the pan for 5 to 10 minutes before serving.

TECHNIQUE TIP: Wear disposable gloves or kitchen gloves when handling the jalapeños or make sure to wash your hands really well after cutting and coring them.

Per Serving (2 halves): Calories: 91; Fat: 4g; Saturated Fat: 2g; Cholesterol: 0mg; Carbohydrates: 9g; Fiber: 2g; Protein: 5g; Sodium: 305mg

Cheesy Bowtie Crackers

NUT-FREE, SOY-FREE, CROWD-PLEASER

SERVES: 4 | **PREP TIME:** 15 minutes, plus 30 minutes
cooling time | **COOK TIME:** 20 minutes

These crackers are as fun as they are easy to make. You can use any type of gluten-free pasta. I think farfalle works and looks the best, but you could use broken lasagna noodles. Try them dipped in Cashew Ranch Dressing (page 211) or Sunflower Seed Cheese Sauce (page 210).

---

4 cups water

5 tablespoons nutritional yeast, divided

1 tablespoon table salt

1 tablespoon apple cider vinegar

2 cups gluten-free bowtie pasta (farfalle)

1 tablespoon avocado oil

½ teaspoon onion powder

¼ teaspoon garlic powder

---

1. Preheat the oven to 425°F. Line a rimmed baking sheet with parchment.

2. In a large pot, bring the water to a boil and stir in 2 tablespoons of nutritional yeast, the salt, and the vinegar. Add the noodles; cook for 4 minutes. Drain the noodles, but do not rinse. Transfer the noodles back to the pot.

3. Drizzle the oil over the noodles and stir to coat. Sprinkle the remaining 3 tablespoons of nutritional yeast, the onion powder, and the garlic powder over the noodles, stir well, and then spread the noodles out on the prepared baking sheet in a single layer.

4. Bake for 8 minutes, then flip the noodles and move the ones from the center to the edges of the pan. Bake for 8 more minutes or until the crackers are browning on the edges.

5. Remove from the oven and transfer the crackers to a wire rack to cool to room temperature, about 30 minutes. They will crisp up more as they cool.

6. Store the crackers in an airtight container on the counter for up to 2 days.

Per Serving: Calories: 246; Fat: 5g; Saturated Fat: 1g; Cholesterol: 0mg; Carbohydrates: 45g; Fiber: 7g; Protein: 7g; Sodium: 693mg

Corn Dog–Style Baby Carrots

NUT-FREE, SOY-FREE, CROWD-PLEASER

SERVES: 8 | **PREP TIME:** 20 minutes, plus 1 hour marinating and
10 minutes cooling time | **COOK TIME:** 20 minutes

You don't need to go to the state fair to enjoy these corn dogs. In this vegan and gluten-free variety, carrots are marinated in spices and liquid smoke and then rolled in a cornmeal dough. The carrots' natural sweetness paired with the smoky marinade makes them a great complement to the crispy corn dog coating. You can also use firm tofu for the center if you're looking to add protein.

---

1 cup boiling water

1 tablespoon liquid smoke

¼ cup coconut aminos

1 teaspoon paprika

1 teaspoon onion powder

1 (16-ounce) package baby carrots

1 cup 1:1 all-purpose gluten-free flour, homemade (page 206) or store-bought

1 cup yellow cornmeal

1 teaspoon baking powder

½ teaspoon table salt

½ teaspoon ground mustard

6 tablespoons vegan butter

½ cup unsweetened gluten-free nondairy milk, homemade (page 218) or store-bought

¼ cup pure maple syrup

Nonstick cooking spray

---

1. In a small bowl, whisk together the water, liquid smoke, coconut aminos, paprika, and onion powder. Mix in the baby carrots, cover with a lid or aluminum foil, and let marinate for an hour. For even better results, marinate the carrots overnight.

2. Preheat the oven to 400°F. Line a large rimmed baking sheet with parchment paper. Set aside.

3. Drain the carrots in a colander but do not rinse. Leave the colander in the sink while you prepare the dough.

4. In a mixing bowl, whisk together the flour, cornmeal, baking powder, salt, and ground mustard. Using a pastry cutter or forks, cut the butter into the dry mixture until it looks like little pebbles. Stir in the milk and maple syrup using a heavy wooden spoon.

5. Turn the dough out onto a sheet of parchment paper. Place another sheet on top. Roll out the dough to a ¼-inch thickness. Use the carrots as a guide for how big to cut the dough. The dough should be able to wrap around the carrot so that it evenly covers it. Once the dough is cut, use your hands to press the dough firmly around the carrots.

6. Place the prepared corn dogs on the parchment-lined baking sheet and spray them with a little cooking spray. Bake for 15 minutes, turn the corn dogs, spray with a little more cooking spray, and then bake for 5 more minutes. Remove the corn dogs from the oven; allow them to cool for 10 minutes before enjoying.

INGREDIENT SMARTS: You can use standard carrots cut into chunks for this recipe, but make sure they aren't too thick or they won't cook fully through.

Per Serving: Calories: 283; Fat: 10g; Saturated Fat: 2g; Cholesterol: 0mg; Carbohydrates: 44g; Fiber: 4g; Protein: 5g; Sodium: 450mg

Plantain Chips with Lime Yogurt Sauce

NUT-FREE, SOY-FREE, CROWD-PLEASER

SERVES: 4 | **PREP TIME:** 20 minutes | **COOK TIME:** 20 minutes

Unlike their sweet relative, the banana, plantains make a satisfyingly savory chip that pairs perfectly with a zesty lime yogurt sauce. Store-bought plantain chips often come coated in sugar and a list of artificial ingredients, and they are really expensive. Making them at home dramatically cuts down on cost and gives you control over the ingredients. These are a great appetizer or side dish for a veggie burger.

---

1 cup plain, unsweetened nondairy yogurt

¼ cup chopped fresh cilantro

1 teaspoon ground cumin

Juice of 1 lime

½ teaspoon table salt

2 large light green plantains, peeled (see Ingredient Smarts tip)

1 tablespoon avocado oil

1 teaspoon kosher salt

---

1. In a small bowl, mix together the yogurt, cilantro, cumin, lime juice, and salt. Cover the bowl and refrigerate until ready to serve.

2. Preheat the oven to 350°F. Line a large rimmed baking sheet with parchment paper. Set aside.

3. Using a sharp knife, slice both plantains into thin coins or skinny strips, approximately ⅛ inch thick.

4. Put the sliced plantains in a large bowl and drizzle with the oil. Use your hands to thoroughly and gently coat the plantains in the oil.

5. Lay out the plantain slices in a single layer on the prepared baking sheet and sprinkle with the salt.

6. Bake for 15 minutes, flip, and then bake for 5 more minutes. The edges of the plantains should be golden brown. Remove the baking sheet from the oven; transfer the chips to a wire rack. As they cool completely, they will crisp up more.

INGREDIENT SMARTS: Plantains may look like bananas, but how you select them is completely different. A ripe plantain has a nearly black peel but is still somewhat firm to the touch. This recipe calls for slightly green, almost yellow plantains so the chips aren't too sweet or soft.

Per Serving: Calories: 210; Fat: 5g; Saturated Fat: 1g; Cholesterol: 0mg; Carbohydrates: 42g; Fiber: 3g; Protein: 3g; Sodium: 885mg

Pineapple-Turmeric-Ginger Lemonade

NUT-FREE, SOY-FREE, CROWD-PLEASER, WHOLE-FOOD PLANT-BASED

MAKES: 8 cups | **PREP TIME:** 15 minutes, plus 1 hour cooling | **COOK TIME:** 25 minutes

The ingredients in this refreshing, slightly spicy drink are all known for their anti-inflammatory properties. Not only is this vibrant lemonade great for warm summer afternoons, but it also makes a great post-workout drink, and you don't have to juice any lemons!

---

6 cups water

1 cup peeled and chopped fresh ginger (about a 6-inch knob)

6 lemons, washed and quartered, plus lemon slices for serving (optional)

½ pineapple, peeled, flesh and core chopped

1½ teaspoons ground turmeric

¼ teaspoon freshly ground black pepper

½ cup agave syrup

Mint, for serving (optional)

---

1. In a large pot over medium-high heat, add the water and bring it to a boil. Add the ginger, reduce the heat to medium-low, cover, and simmer for 10 minutes.

2. Turn off the heat and add the quartered lemons and pineapple. Cover and let the mixture steep for 15 minutes. Add the turmeric and black pepper, and mix with a heavy spoon, pressing on the pineapple and lemons to extract their juices. Strain the steeped liquid through a fine-mesh strainer into a heatproof pitcher. Press the lemons and pineapple lightly into the strainer to remove more juice. Stir the agave syrup into the strained lemonade, and refrigerate for at least 1 hour before serving.

3. Serve over ice, garnished with a slice of lemon and a few mint leaves, if using. Store in the refrigerator in a covered pitcher for up to 1 week; wait to add the mint leaves and lemon slices until serving.

Per Serving (1 cup): Calories: 70; Fat: 0g; Saturated Fat: 0g; Cholesterol: 0mg; Carbohydrates: 19g; Fiber: 0g; Protein: 0g; Sodium: 14mg

Homemade Masala Chai

NUT-FREE, SOY-FREE, 30 MINUTES, CROWD-PLEASER,
WHOLE-FOOD PLANT-BASED

SERVES: 4 | **PREP TIME:** 10 minutes | **COOK TIME:** 15 minutes

Homemade chai is very different than the syrup blend you can purchase in stores. Masala chai, meaning "spiced tea," is highly fragrant with some lingering heat from cardamom and ginger—less sweet and more flavorful.

---

6 green cardamom pods

1 teaspoon whole peppercorns

1 (½-inch) piece fresh ginger, peeled and cut into pea-sized pieces

15 whole cloves

4 cinnamon sticks

¾ teaspoon ground nutmeg

4 cups water

2 tablespoons loose leaf black tea

2 cups unsweetened gluten-free nondairy milk, homemade (page 218) or store-bought

3 to 4 tablespoons pure maple syrup

1 teaspoon pure vanilla extract

---

1. Slightly crush the cardamom pods and peppercorns using a mortar and pestle or 2 nesting bowls. The goal is to split open the cardamom pods.

2. In a stock pot, combine the cardamom, peppercorns, ginger, cloves, cinnamon sticks, nutmeg, and water. Bring the water to a boil, reduce the heat, cover, and simmer for 5 minutes. Turn off the heat and add the black tea. Stir, cover, and let steep for 5 minutes.

3. Strain the tea through a fine-mesh strainer or a cheesecloth-lined colander into a heatproof pitcher or another pot. Rinse the pot, transfer the strained liquid back to the pot, and stir in the milk, maple syrup, and vanilla. Heat to a simmer for immediate drinking, or store the tea in a bottle in your refrigerator to be reheated when desired. It will keep for up to 1 week.

MAKE AHEAD: Add the milk mixture just before you're ready to drink the chai. That way, the premade flavored water (with no milk added) will last in the refrigerator for up to 2 weeks.

Per Serving: Calories: 88; Fat: 0g; Saturated Fat: 0g; Cholesterol: 2mg; Carbohydrates: 16g; Fiber: 0g; Protein: 4g; Sodium: 66mg

Loaded Potato Skins

NUT-FREE, CROWD-PLEASER

MAKES: 10 potato skins | **PREP TIME:** 30 minutes, plus cooling time | **COOK TIME:** 50 minutes

Potato skins are easy to make, fun to look at, and memorably delicious. Most restaurant-style potato skins are deep-fried, topped, and then broiled. Delicious, yes, but unhealthy. These potato skins are baked until crisp, loaded with mashed potatoes, tempeh bacon, and vegan cream cheese, and then baked again with a sprinkle of vegan cheddar cheese or a drizzle of Sunflower Seed Cheese Sauce (page 210).

---

5 small russet potatoes

4 tablespoons unsalted vegan butter, melted, divided

½ teaspoon dried parsley

¼ teaspoon seasoned salt

¼ teaspoon garlic powder

¼ cup unsweetened gluten-free nondairy milk, homemade (page 218) or store-bought

¼ cup vegan cream cheese, at room temperature

4 ounces tempeh, crumbled (⅔ cup)

1 teaspoon liquid smoke

1 teaspoon smoked paprika

1 cup shredded vegan cheddar cheese

2 tablespoons chopped chives

Vegan sour cream, or Cashew Ranch Dressing (page 211), for serving (optional)

---

1. Use a fork to poke holes in the potatoes and, working in batches of 1 or 2 potatoes at a time, microwave on high for 5 to 7 minutes, until tender. If you don't have a microwave, preheat the oven to 425°F, poke holes in the potatoes using a fork, place them on a baking sheet, and bake for 45 to 60 minutes, until tender. Let the potatoes cool completely.

2. Preheat the oven to 425°F. Line a large rimmed baking sheet with parchment paper. Set aside.

3. In a small bowl, combine 2 tablespoons melted butter, the parsley, seasoned salt, and garlic powder. Set aside.

4. Cut the potatoes in half lengthwise. Using a small spoon, scoop out the flesh, leaving a ¼-inch-thick shell. Place the baked potato flesh in a small bowl (or in the bowl of a stand mixer) and add the remaining 2 tablespoons of melted butter, the milk, and the cream cheese. Mix to combine.

5. Brush the inside and outside of the potatoes with the melted butter–parsley mixture. Place the potato skins cut-side down on the prepared baking sheet. Bake for 15 minutes, flip the skins over, and then bake for an additional 5 minutes.

6. While the potato skins bake, prepare the tempeh. Heat a medium nonstick frying pan over medium-high heat. Cook the crumbled tempeh with the liquid smoke and paprika for 10 minutes, stirring occasionally and breaking up the tempeh with a spoon. Remove the frying pan from the heat and set aside.

7. Fill each potato skin with the mashed potato mixture, then the tempeh, and top with a sprinkle of cheddar cheese. Bake for 5 minutes or until the cheese is melted and bubbly.

8. Remove the potato skins from the oven, top with chives, and serve with dollops of sour cream, if using.

MAKE AHEAD: You can make the baked potatoes up to a week in advance and store them in an airtight container in the refrigerator.

Per Serving (2 skins): Calories: 389; Fat: 20g; Saturated Fat: 8g; Cholesterol: 0mg; Carbohydrates: 36g; Fiber: 7g; Protein: 17g; Sodium: 741mg

Soft Pretzel Bites with Beer Cheese

NUT-FREE, SOY-FREE, CROWD-PLEASER

SERVES: 8 | **PREP TIME:** 30 minutes, plus 1 hour rising time and 30 minutes resting time | **COOK TIME:** 20 minutes

These homemade pretzel bites are ready to party. Learn to make pretzels the traditional way: by first boiling the shaped dough in alkaline water to give them that distinctive chewy crust, then baking them to brown the exterior while making the inside pillowy soft. Serve the pretzel bites with this delectable vegan beer cheese dip and/or mustard for a more classic twist.

FOR THE PRETZELS

- 3 cups 1:1 all-purpose gluten-free flour, homemade (page 206) or store-bought
- 1 tablespoon instant dry yeast
- 1 tablespoon vegan brown sugar
- 1 teaspoon kosher salt, plus more for topping
- 1 tablespoon psyllium husk powder (see Ingredient Smarts tip)
- 3 tablespoons avocado oil
- 1¼ cups unsweetened gluten-free nondairy milk, homemade (page 218) or store-bought
- 1 teaspoon apple cider vinegar
- 6 cups water
- ½ cup baking soda

FOR THE BEER CHEESE DIP (OPTIONAL)

- 8 ounces vegan cream cheese, softened
- 8 ounces vegan cheddar cheese, shredded
- 1 tablespoon Dijon mustard
- 2 garlic cloves, minced
- ½ teaspoon onion powder
- ½ cup gluten-free pale ale beer
- 2 teaspoons cornstarch

1. To make the pretzels: In a large bowl, whisk together the flour, yeast, brown sugar, salt, and psyllium husk. Pour in the oil, milk, and vinegar. Mix with a heavy spoon until the dough comes together, then knead it in the bowl or on a lightly floured countertop for about 5 minutes, until the dough is smooth and free of visible lumps. Add more flour as needed so the dough doesn't stick to your hands. Mixing and kneading can also be done using a stand mixer with a dough hook attachment. Transfer the dough to a lightly oiled bowl, cover, and let rise at room temperature for 1 hour.

2. While the dough rises, make the beer cheese dip (if desired): In a blender or food processor, puree the cream cheese, cheddar cheese, mustard, garlic, onion powder, beer, and cornstarch. Pour the mixture into a saucepan over medium-high heat, and cook, stirring constantly, until the mixture is bubbling and the cheese has melted. Remove the pan from the heat. Transfer the dip to an airtight container and place it in the refrigerator to chill, or leave it in the pan to reheat and serve warm later.

3. Preheat the oven to 450°F. Line 2 large rimmed baking sheets with parchment paper.

4. Divide the dough into 4 equal parts. Roll each piece into a ball, then into a long rope that is roughly 1 inch in diameter. Cut the long ropes into 2-inch pieces; place the bites on the prepared baking sheets. Cover with plastic wrap and let the dough rest for 30 minutes.

5. Meanwhile, in a large pot, bring the water to a boil with the baking soda. When the dough pieces are finished resting, drop them into the water, 10 to 12 pieces at a time, and boil for 1 minute, gently flipping the pretzels in the water periodically.

6. Transfer to parchment paper, top with kosher salt to taste, and bake for 12 to 15 minutes, until golden brown. Serve the pretzel bites with chilled or warm beer cheese sauce.

MAKE AHEAD: You can make the dough 1 day ahead of time. Either let it rise overnight in the refrigerator (step 1), or cover and refrigerate the bite-size dough pieces on the baking sheet. If the dough is shaped, you can go right from the fridge to the boiling water (step 5), which will save you time if you're serving a crowd. This dough can also be shaped into standard (2-by-3-inch) pretzels.

INGREDIENT SMARTS: Psyllium husk powder can be used in baking to mimic gluten. It can be found in the baking, health food, or supplement aisle at the grocery store.

Per Serving: Calories: 286; Fat: 6g; Saturated Fat: 1g; Cholesterol: 1mg; Carbohydrates: 51g; Fiber: 2g; Protein: 5g; Sodium: 1,069mg

Savory Sorghum Crackers

NUT-FREE, SOY-FREE

MAKES: 32 crackers | **PREP TIME:** 15 minutes, plus 30 minutes
cooling time | **COOK TIME:** 45 minutes

This Scandinavian-inspired savory cracker, known as Knækbrød, is traditionally made using rye flour, seeds, nori, and spices. Here, the umami flavor of the nori complements the natural sweetness of sorghum flour, making a distinctly savory cracker that pairs well with sweet spreads, fresh fruit, and vegan cheese spreads.

2 teaspoons fennel seeds	1 cup sorghum flour	2 tablespoons poppy seeds
1 teaspoon cumin seeds, not ground	1 teaspoon xanthan gum	½ teaspoon onion powder
	¼ cup chia seeds	¾ teaspoon kosher salt
1 large sheet nori	¼ cup sunflower seeds	¼ cup extra-virgin olive oil
1 cup gluten-free oats	¼ cup pumpkin seeds	¾ cup water

1. Preheat the oven to 350°F.

2. Using a mortar and pestle, crush the fennel and cumin seeds just to open them up; do not grind them completely.

3. Crumble the nori into a large bowl. Add the crushed spices, oats, flour, xanthan gum, chia seeds, sunflower seeds, pumpkin seeds, poppy seeds, onion powder, salt, oil, and water. Mix well; the dough will be sticky.

4. Place half of the dough on a piece of parchment paper. Place another parchment sheet on top. Roll the dough very thin, about ⅛ inch thick, peel off the top layer of parchment, and place the dough with the bottom layer of parchment paper on a large rimmed baking sheet. Repeat this process with the other half of the dough and a second baking sheet.

5. Using a sharp knife, lightly score each sheet of dough into 16 (1-by-2-inch) squares. Bake for 15 minutes, swap the baking sheets between the oven racks (this helps the crackers bake evenly), and bake for 15 minutes more, until the crackers are browned. Rotate again between oven racks, and bake for a final 15 minutes.

6. Remove the baking sheets from the oven. Let the crackers cool on the baking sheets for about 30 minutes, then break them apart. The crackers will crisp up as they cool, and they can be stored in an airtight container on the counter for up to 1 week.

TECHNIQUE TIP: If you do not have a mortar and pestle, you can place the whole fennel and cumin seeds on a baking sheet or glass dish and use the bottom of a cup or bowl to carefully press down on them. The fennel and cumin seeds need to be cracked and not ground, so you do not need to press hard to open them.

Per Serving (4 crackers): Calories: 263; Fat: 15g; Saturated Fat: 2g; Cholesterol: 0mg; Carbohydrates: 26g; Fiber: 6g; Protein: 7g; Sodium: 232mg

CHAPTER 4

Salads, Sandwiches, and Soups

Peach and Basil Caprese Salad

NUT-FREE, CROWD-PLEASER

SERVES: 4 | **PREP TIME:** 15 minutes, plus overnight marinating time

Here, firm tofu is marinated overnight in a seasoned brine and served with fresh peach slices, which add a little natural sweetness, mimicking the classic combo of tomatoes and mozzarella. Make extra tofu for snacking, sandwiches, or salads.

---

1 (14-ounce) package firm tofu

3 tablespoons white balsamic vinegar

¼ cup kosher salt, plus more for sprinkling

2 tablespoons nutritional yeast

2 teaspoons arrowroot powder

2 cups unsweetened gluten-free nondairy milk, homemade (page 218) or store-bought

2 large peaches, pitted and sliced

1 cup packed fresh basil leaves

Freshly ground black pepper

1 tablespoon balsamic reduction (optional)

---

1. Cut the tofu into 2-inch squares that are approximately ¼ inch thick. Place the cut tofu on a paper towel–lined plate while you prepare the other ingredients.

2. In an 8-by-8-inch baking dish, whisk together the vinegar, salt, nutritional yeast, arrowroot powder, and milk. Place the tofu into the baking dish and add more milk as necessary to cover the tofu. Cover the dish and refrigerate for 8 to 24 hours. Drain it, pat the tofu dry, and sprinkle with salt.

3. Layer the peach slices, marinated tofu, and basil leaves. Top with freshly ground black pepper and a drizzle of balsamic reduction, if desired.

INGREDIENT SMARTS: White balsamic, not the standard brown variety, is essential. It is a touch sweeter, and the clear color does not turn the tofu brown. It is a good ingredient to have on hand to season roasted veggies or to make vibrant vinaigrettes.

Per Serving: Calories: 246; Fat: 9g; Saturated Fat: 2g; Cholesterol: 0mg; Carbohydrates: 23g; Fiber: 4g; Protein: 22g; Sodium: 596mg

Wedge Salad with Gluten-Free Croutons

30 MINUTES

SERVES: 4 | **PREP TIME:** 20 minutes | **COOK TIME:** 6 to 10 minutes

Wedge salad is crisp, refreshing, and so easy to make, creating the perfect complement to just about any meal. Don't skip the fresh croutons; they're delightfully crispy, and you can season them however you like.

---

2 gluten-free burger buns, homemade (page 202) or store-bought

1 tablespoon extra-virgin olive oil

1 teaspoon Italian seasoning

1 head iceberg lettuce, cut into quarters, core removed

1 cup vegan and gluten-free ranch dressing, homemade (page 211) or store-bought, plus more for serving

4 slices Tempeh "Bacon" (page 212), crumbled

1 cup cherry tomatoes, halved

2 tablespoons chopped fresh chives

---

1. Cut the burger buns into ½-inch cubes. In a medium bowl, toss the bread with the oil, then sprinkle with the Italian seasoning.

2. Heat a small nonstick frying pan over medium heat. Add the oiled bread cubes to the pan and spread them out in a single layer. Cook for 3 minutes, flip them, and cook for another 3 minutes. Continue to flip and cook until all sides are browned. Remove from the heat.

3. Divide the lettuce wedges among individual plates, and top them with the dressing, tempeh bacon, tomatoes, chives, and croutons.

Per Serving: Calories: 611; Fat: 31g; Saturated Fat: 6g; Cholesterol: 0mg; Carbohydrates: 62g; Fiber: 8g; Protein: 24g; Sodium: 532mg

Sunflower Seed "Tuna" Sandwiches

NUT-FREE, SOY-FREE, WHOLE-FOOD PLANT-BASED

SERVES: 4 | **PREP TIME:** 10 minutes, plus overnight soaking time

Heart-healthy raw sunflower seeds take center stage for this recipe. Soaking and then pulsing them in a food processor gives them a fine, tuna-like texture, and the nori adds a taste of the sea.

---

2 cups raw sunflower seeds

3 cups low-sodium mushroom stock or vegetable stock

¼ cup pickle juice (I prefer dill pickle juice)

2 full sheets nori, finely chopped

1 tablespoon apple cider vinegar

½ small red onion, diced

1 tablespoon dried dill

¼ cup Dijon mustard

Table salt

Freshly ground black pepper

4 gluten-free pitas, tortillas, or buns

Microgreens, watercress, spinach, or arugula, for serving

---

1. In a medium bowl, combine the sunflower seeds and the stock; cover and refrigerate overnight.

2. The next day, drain the sunflower seeds, then place them in a food processor with the pickle juice, nori, vinegar, onion, and dill. Pulse until the seeds are mostly broken up and combined but not smooth.

3. Transfer the mixture to a medium bowl. Fold in the mustard, taste, and season with salt and pepper as desired.

4. Serve the "tuna" salad on gluten-free pitas with greens.

CHANGE IT UP: You can swap out the sunflower seeds in this recipe for 2 (15-ounce) cans of chickpeas. Drain and rinse the chickpeas, and then, instead of putting them through a food processor, simply mash them with a potato masher until they are crumbly and broken down.

Per Serving: Calories: 637; Fat: 41g; Saturated Fat: 4g; Cholesterol: 0mg; Carbohydrates: 45g; Fiber: 9g; Protein: 22g; Sodium: 625mg

Chickpea Caesar Salad Wrap

ESSENTIAL RECIPE, NUT-FREE, 30 MINUTES

SERVES: 4 | **PREP TIME:** 15 minutes

Caesar salad is one of those sneaky non-vegan menu options because the sauce is usually made with anchovies. This recipe builds a similar flavor using green olives, capers, and vegan Worcestershire sauce. Mixed with silken tofu, it makes a delicious, creamy salad dressing. Add lightly mashed chickpeas, and you have a flavorful wrap that is nutrient-dense and delicious.

---

1 (12-ounce) container soft silken tofu

2 tablespoons freshly squeezed lemon juice

2 tablespoons extra-virgin olive oil

1 tablespoon Dijon mustard

1 teaspoon vegan Worcestershire sauce

2 garlic cloves, crushed

2 teaspoons nutritional yeast

1 teaspoon table salt

1 teaspoon freshly ground black pepper

1 (15-ounce) can chickpeas, drained

2 tablespoons capers

¼ cup chopped green olives

4 gluten-free wraps

2 romaine lettuce leaves, chopped

2 Roma tomatoes, diced

---

1. In a food processor, puree the tofu, lemon juice, oil, mustard, Worcestershire sauce, garlic, nutritional yeast, salt, and pepper. Scrape the sides to ensure all ingredients are blended into the sauce.

2. In a small bowl, mash the chickpeas using a potato masher or heavy spoon until they are just broken down but not smooth. Add the tofu mixture, mix well, and then fold in the capers and olives.

3. Serve in gluten-free wraps with lettuce and tomato.

INGREDIENT SMARTS: The most easy-to-find brand of vegan Worcestershire sauce is The Wizard's Organic, which is stocked in the natural foods section of many grocery stores.

Per Serving: Calories: 279; Fat: 13g; Saturated Fat: 2g; Cholesterol: 0mg; Carbohydrates: 32g; Fiber: 7g; Protein: 12g; Sodium: 936mg

Crispy Hearts of Palm Po' Boy

NUT-FREE, SOY-FREE, 30 MINUTES, CROWD-PLEASER

SERVES: 4 | **PREP TIME:** 30 minutes, not including
Remoulade Sauce | **COOK TIME:** 10 minutes

Hearts of palm have become a popular vegan substitute for seafood recipes because their texture is surprisingly similar to scallops and shrimp. The neutral-flavored vegetable takes on any seasoning, too, and when breaded and fried or baked, it makes a great vegan version of the famous Louisiana po' boy sandwich.

---

1 cup coconut flour, divided

2 tablespoons
arrowroot powder

½ cup aquafaba (the liquid
from a can of chickpeas)

1 cup unsweetened
gluten-free nondairy milk,
homemade (page 218) or
store-bought

2 tablespoons chili powder

2 tablespoons
smoked paprika

1 teaspoon cayenne pepper
(optional)

1 tablespoon garlic powder

4 cups gluten-free panko
breadcrumbs

Avocado or safflower oil,
for frying

2 (14-ounce) cans hearts
of palm, drained and
patted dry

Table salt

Freshly ground
black pepper

4 gluten-free burger buns,
homemade (page 202) or
store-bought

Shredded lettuce,
for topping

1 Roma tomato, sliced

1 recipe Southern-Style
Remoulade Sauce
(page 217)

---

1. In a small bowl, mix ½ cup of coconut flour, arrowroot powder, aquafaba, and milk until well combined. Stir in the chili powder, smoked paprika, cayenne, if using, and garlic powder. Put the remaining ½ cup of coconut flour in a second small bowl. Put the panko breadcrumbs in a third small bowl.

2. In a medium saucepan or pot, heat roughly 1 inch of oil over medium heat.

3. Cut the hearts of palm into ½-inch coins, roughly 6 pieces per stalk. Dip the pieces into the coconut flour, then the wet mixture, and lastly into the panko.

4. Fry the coated hearts of palm at medium heat for about 4 minutes on each side, until the panko is golden brown. Transfer the fried hearts of palm pieces to a paper towel–lined plate or dish; sprinkle with salt and pepper to taste.

5. Serve on gluten-free burger buns topped with lettuce, tomato slices, and remoulade sauce.

INGREDIENT SMARTS: Aquafaba, liquid from canned chickpeas, is a versatile ingredient that you'll find yourself using more and more as a gluten-free, vegan cook. It works as an egg replacer for cake and muffin recipes, as well as batters. The best part is that it's a free ingredient. When you make a recipe with chickpeas, make sure to save the liquid for future uses. It can be frozen for long-term storage or refrigerated in an airtight container for up to 1 week.

Per Serving: Calories: 968; Fat: 37g; Saturated Fat: 4g; Cholesterol: 1mg; Carbohydrates: 127g; Fiber: 23g; Protein: 28g; Sodium: 1,054mg

Eggplant Bacon "E-L-T"

NUT-FREE, SOY-FREE

SERVES: 4 | **PREP TIME:** 15 minutes, plus 10 minutes cooling time | **COOK TIME:** 45 minutes

Eggplant is a versatile vegetable because it can be seasoned in a variety of ways and cooked or baked to create many different textures. Here, thin strips of eggplant are seasoned and baked to make a crisp and flavorful bacon substitute for a vegan take on the BLT.

---

1 medium eggplant, peeled and cut into thin strips

¼ cup coconut aminos

3 tablespoons agave syrup

¼ cup liquid smoke

2 tablespoons tahini

2 tablespoons apple cider vinegar

2 teaspoons paprika

2 teaspoons garlic powder

1 teaspoon ground cumin

1 teaspoon kosher salt

4 gluten-free burger buns, homemade (page 202) or store-bought

Vegan mayo, for serving

2 romaine lettuce leaves, chopped

2 beefsteak tomatoes, sliced

---

1. Preheat the oven to 275°F. Line 2 large rimmed baking sheets with parchment paper.

2. Place the eggplant slices in a single layer on the prepared baking sheets.

3. In a large glass or metal bowl, mix together the coconut aminos, agave syrup, liquid smoke, tahini, vinegar, paprika, garlic powder, and cumin. Brush the eggplant strips on both sides with this mixture.

4. Bake the eggplant strips for 45 minutes, flipping them halfway through the baking time, until the strips are crispy on the edges. Remove the eggplant from the oven and immediately sprinkle it with the salt. Let the eggplant cool on the baking sheet for 10 minutes.

5. To assemble the E-L-T sandwiches, slather gluten-free buns with vegan mayo, then add slices of eggplant bacon, lettuce, and tomato.

Per Serving: Calories: 282; Fat: 5g; Saturated Fat: 1g; Cholesterol: 1mg; Carbohydrates: 54g; Fiber: 2g; Protein: 5g; Sodium: 254mg

Coconut Corn Chowder

NUT-FREE, SOY-FREE, WHOLE-FOOD PLANT-BASED

SERVES: 4 | **PREP TIME:** 15 minutes | **COOK TIME:** 20 minutes

Corn chowder is creamy and naturally sweet, but it can also be rather bland. This recipe elevates the standard soup with a little heat and everybody's favorite ingredient—coconut milk. A sprinkle of coconut, peanuts, and some fresh cilantro help this soup come alive.

2 shallots, thinly sliced

3 roasted garlic cloves, mashed (see Mashed Cauliflower and Rutabaga with Roasted Garlic, page 102, for ingredient tip)

1 tablespoon grated fresh ginger

1 jalapeño, seeded and minced, or 1 (4-ounce) can green chiles

2 tablespoons water, divided

5 cups frozen corn kernels

1 large sweet potato, peeled and cut into ½-inch cubes

3 cups low-sodium vegetable stock

1 (15-ounce) can full-fat coconut milk

1 tablespoon freshly squeezed lime juice

Kosher salt

Lime wedges, for serving

Toasted unsweetened coconut flakes, for garnish (optional)

Chopped peanuts, for garnish (optional)

Torn fresh cilantro, for garnish (optional)

1. In a large stockpot over medium heat, combine the shallots, roasted garlic, ginger, jalapeño, and 1 tablespoon of water. Cook for 3 minutes, stirring occasionally, until the shallots are soft and the mixture is fragrant. Add the other tablespoon of water if the garlic starts to brown. Add the corn and sauté until the kernels thaw and brighten in color, about 3 minutes.

2. Stir in the sweet potato and stock. Bring to a boil, reduce the heat to medium-low, cover the pot, and cook for 10 minutes or until the sweet potato is soft.

3. Use an immersion blender to coarsely puree the soup. Stir in the coconut milk and lime juice, and heat until the soup starts to bubble around the edges.

4. Season with salt to taste; serve with lime wedges and any optional garnishes.

Per Serving: Calories: 478; Fat: 25g; Saturated Fat: 20g; Cholesterol: 0mg; Carbohydrates: 58g; Fiber: 6g; Protein: 9g; Sodium: 79mg

Samosa Wrap

NUT-FREE, SOY-FREE, WHOLE-FOOD PLANT-BASED

SERVES: 4 | **PREP TIME:** 15 minutes | **COOK TIME:** 11 minutes

This wrap is inspired by a popular Indian appetizer. You can serve this samosa filling hot or cold, on a salad, or over a serving of rice, too.

FOR THE FILLING

2 medium russet potatoes, peeled and roughly chopped

1 tablespoon water

2 teaspoons ground coriander

1 teaspoon ground cumin

1 teaspoon ground turmeric

½ teaspoon cayenne pepper

½ teaspoon garlic powder

½ teaspoon kosher salt

2 teaspoons grated fresh ginger

1 (4-ounce) can diced mild green chiles

1 cup frozen peas, thawed

1 (15-ounce) can chickpeas, drained

FOR THE CHUTNEY

3 tablespoons chopped fresh mint

2 tablespoons chopped fresh cilantro

1 teaspoon freshly squeezed lemon juice

1 tablespoon grated fresh ginger

FOR THE WRAPS

4 gluten-free wraps

1 Roma tomato, diced

Chopped fresh cilantro, for garnish

1. To make the filling: Place the potatoes in a medium saucepan, cover them with water, bring to a boil over high heat, then cook for 5 minutes. Drain, transfer the potatoes to a medium bowl, and mash them until there are still some small chunks visible.

2. In a large nonstick skillet over medium-high heat, combine the water, spices, and salt. Cook for 30 seconds. Stir in the ginger and chiles, cook for 30 seconds, and then fold in the potatoes, peas, and chickpeas. Remove the pan from the heat, cover and let it sit for 5 minutes.

3. To make the chutney: Stir together the herbs, lemon juice, and ginger.

4. To assemble the wraps: Divide the filling, chutney, tomato, and cilantro between the wraps, then fold to serve.

Per Serving: Calories: 260; Fat: 3g; Saturated Fat: 0g; Cholesterol: 0mg; Carbohydrates: 52g; Fiber: 9g; Protein: 10g; Sodium: 314mg

Balsamic Mushroom and Quinoa Lettuce Wraps

SOY-FREE, 30 MINUTES, WHOLE-FOOD PLANT-BASED

SERVES: 4 | **PREP TIME:** 15 minutes | **COOK TIME:** 10 minutes, not including quinoa cooking time

Lettuce wraps are a great way to get in an extra serving of vegetables, and they're naturally gluten-free. This wrap is filled with a mix of quinoa and mushrooms, flavored with a balsamic reduction, and served with raw veggies.

8 ounces cremini mushrooms, chopped

1 tablespoon coconut aminos

1 lime

1 cup cooked tri-color quinoa

1 teaspoon seasoned rice vinegar

¼ cup chopped scallions (green parts only)

8 leaves romaine lettuce

½ English cucumber, cut into strips

1 large carrot, julienned

¼ cup crushed peanuts

1 tablespoon balsamic reduction

1. Place the mushrooms in a medium skillet over medium heat. Cook for 3 minutes without stirring, then pour the coconut aminos over the mushrooms, flip them, and cook for 5 minutes longer, until there is a slight blackening on the edges. Squeeze the lime over the mushrooms and stir in the quinoa. Sprinkle on the vinegar, remove the pan from the heat, and top with the scallions.

2. Spoon the filling into the lettuce leaves, then top with the cucumber, carrot, and peanuts. Drizzle with the balsamic reduction. Tightly wrap the leaves around the filling and serve.

MAKE AHEAD: Cook the quinoa ahead to make this meal come together quickly. Bring 1 cup of water or vegetable stock to a boil, stir in ⅓ cup of dry quinoa, reduce to a simmer, cover, and cook for 20 minutes. Keep the cooked quinoa in the refrigerator for up to 1 week.

Per Serving: Calories: 138; Fat: 6g; Saturated Fat: 1g; Cholesterol: 0mg; Carbohydrates: 17g; Fiber: 4g; Protein: 6g; Sodium: 89mg

Simple Tomato Soup

NUT-FREE, SOY-FREE, 30 MINUTES, CROWD-PLEASER,
WHOLE-FOOD PLANT-BASED

SERVES: 4 | **PREP TIME:** 10 minutes | **COOK TIME:** 20 minutes

This cozy soup might cue up some nostalgia. The recipe only takes about 30 minutes total to make, and the end result is a flavorful soup that is loaded with vitamins, minerals, and fiber. The addition of sweet potato may seem odd, but it gives the soup a thick, creamy texture, some natural sweetness, and superfood-status health benefits.

---

1 medium sweet potato, peeled and diced

1 medium yellow onion, chopped

4 garlic cloves, chopped

½ cup water

3 tablespoons tomato paste

2 cups low-sodium vegetable stock

1 (28-ounce) can crushed tomatoes

½ teaspoon dried thyme

1 teaspoon dried parsley

Table salt

Freshly ground black pepper

Fresh herbs like parsley, celery leaves or thyme, for garnish (optional)

Gluten-free croutons, for garnish (optional)

---

1. In a large pot, combine the sweet potato and water, bring to a boil over high heat, cover, and reduce the heat to medium. Cook for 5 minutes. The sweet potato should be softened but won't be fully cooked yet. Drain and transfer the sweet potato to a separate bowl and set aside.

2. In the same pot, sauté the onion and garlic over medium-low heat for 3 minutes, adding 1 tablespoon of water at a time to avoid burning or over-browning. The onion should be translucent and just starting to brown.

3. Turn the heat to medium-high and stir in the tomato paste. Cook, stirring, for 30 seconds.

4. Add the cooked sweet potato and the vegetable stock, crushed tomatoes, dried thyme, and parsley. Stir to combine, then bring the liquid to a simmer over medium-high heat. Cover and reduce the heat to medium-low. Cook for 15 minutes, stirring occasionally. If the sweet potato isn't tender enough to be easily pierced with a fork, continue to cook for 5 more minutes.

5. Use an immersion blender to puree the soup right in the pot, or transfer the soup to an upright blender, working in batches. If using an upright blender, make sure to carefully follow the manufacturer's instructions for hot liquids.

6. Add more vegetable stock or water to thin the soup as desired, and reheat it in the pot over low heat if necessary. Serve with salt and pepper to taste, fresh herbs, and/or gluten-free croutons, if desired.

Per Serving: Calories: 85; Fat: 1g; Saturated Fat: 0g; Cholesterol: 0mg; Carbohydrates: 19g; Fiber: 6g; Protein: 3g; Sodium: 294mg

Root Vegetable and Sorghum Stew

NUT-FREE, SOY-FREE, WHOLE-FOOD PLANT-BASED

SERVES: 8 | **PREP TIME:** 20 minutes, plus 10 minutes sitting time | **COOK TIME:** 40 minutes

Sorghum is a lesser-known gluten-free grain, but it deserves more attention, especially because it's perfect in soups and stews. It cooks into a chewy texture that holds up to liquid well, and it is a good gluten-free option for making pilaf. This recipe combines root vegetables, balsamic vinegar, and crushed tomatoes in a rich and flavorful stew.

1 medium rutabaga, peeled and cut into ½-inch cubes

4 medium carrots, cut into ½-inch pieces

1 large yellow onion, diced

4 garlic cloves, minced

1 bay leaf

3 cups water, plus more as needed

1½ cups whole-grain sorghum (see Ingredient Smarts tip)

1 (28-ounce) can crushed tomatoes

4 cups low-sodium vegetable stock, divided

¼ cup balsamic vinegar

1 teaspoon table salt

¼ cup chopped fresh parsley, plus more for garnish

1 teaspoon dried thyme

Freshly ground black pepper, for garnish

1. Preheat the oven to 425°F. Line a large rimmed baking sheet with parchment paper.

2. Place the rutabaga and carrots on the prepared baking sheet in a single layer. Roast for 30 to 35 minutes, flipping halfway through, until the vegetables can be easily pierced with a fork.

3. While the root vegetables roast, in small pot over medium heat, combine the onion, garlic, and bay leaf. Cook for 5 minutes, stirring in 1 tablespoon of water at a time if necessary to avoid scorching. The onion should be lightly browned and soft. Pour in the 3 cups of water and bring to a boil. Stir in the sorghum, reduce the heat to medium-low, cover, and cook for 20 minutes.

4. Add the crushed tomatoes, vegetable stock, balsamic vinegar, and salt to the pot with the cooked sorghum. Bring to a simmer over medium-high heat, then reduce the heat to low. Cook for 10 minutes, until the flavors meld.

5. Stir in the roasted vegetables, parsley, and thyme, turn off the heat, and let the soup sit for 10 minutes before serving. Serve garnished with fresh parsley and a few cracks of black pepper.

INGREDIENT SMARTS: Sorghum, a popular grain in Africa and Asia, is becoming better known in the West due to its impressive nutrient profile. It's rich in vitamins and minerals, like potassium, iron, and B vitamins, plus it is a good source of fiber and protein. It can easily replace rice and quinoa in recipes for a similar texture but nuttier flavor.

Per Serving: Calories: 182; Fat: 2g; Saturated Fat: 0g; Cholesterol: 0mg; Carbohydrates: 40g; Fiber: 7g; Protein: 6g; Sodium: 436mg

Borscht

NUT-FREE, SOY-FREE, WHOLE-FOOD PLANT-BASED

SERVES: 8 | **PREP TIME:** 20 minutes, plus 15 minutes sitting time | **COOK TIME:** 1 hour

Beets, cabbage, carrots, and oyster mushrooms make a vibrant red, sweet-n-sour, nutrient-dense, earthy soup that originally hails from Ukraine. This soup tastes best a day or two later, but it can be served immediately after cooking. The best way to enjoy borscht is with a dollop of vegan sour cream and a sprinkle of fresh dill.

- 4 large red beets (about 1½ pounds), peeled and chopped into ½-inch cubes
- 4 large carrots, peeled and chopped into ½-inch chunks
- 1 large russet potato, scrubbed and cut into ½-inch cubes
- 1 pound oyster mushrooms or cremini mushrooms, chopped
- 1 large yellow onion, chopped
- 8 cups low-sodium vegetable stock, divided
- 2 cups thinly sliced cabbage
- ¾ cup chopped fresh dill, divided
- 3 tablespoons red wine vinegar
- Table salt
- Freshly ground black pepper
- 1 cup vegan sour cream (optional)

---

1. Preheat the oven to 400°F. Line a large rimmed baking sheet with parchment paper.

2. Spread the beets, carrots, and potato on the prepared baking sheet in a single layer. Roast for 20 minutes, until the potatoes are tender and lightly browned.

3. While the vegetables are roasting, heat a large pot over high heat and add the mushrooms and onion. Cook, stirring occasionally, for 10 minutes. The onion and mushrooms should be browned. If they are cooking too quickly, reduce the heat and stir in 1 tablespoon of water at a time, only as needed to prevent burning.

4. Add 4 cups of the vegetable stock and bring to a boil. Add half of the roasted vegetables, reduce the heat to low, cover, and cook for 20 minutes. Add the remaining vegetables and 4 cups stock, the cabbage, and 6 tablespoons of the dill. Bring to a simmer, cover, and cook for 15 minutes to soften the cabbage. Stir in the vinegar and season with salt and freshly ground pepper to taste. Remove the pot from the heat, and let the soup sit for at least 15 minutes before to serving.

5. Serve with the remaining 6 tablespoons of dill as garnish, and top each bowl with a dollop of vegan sour cream, if desired. This soup will deepen in both color and flavor the longer it sits; keep it in an airtight container in the refrigerator for up to 5 days.

Per Serving: Calories: 115; Fat: 1g; Saturated Fat: 0g; Cholesterol: 0mg; Carbohydrates: 25g; Fiber: 6g; Protein: 4g; Sodium: 124mg

Creamy Zuppa Toscana

NUT-FREE, SOY-FREE, CROWD-PLEASER, WHOLE-FOOD PLANT-BASED

SERVES: 8 | **PREP TIME:** 20 minutes | **COOK TIME:** 30 minutes

Classic Italian zuppa Toscana (often known as ribollita) usually involves a mix of tomatoes, cannellini beans, carrots, celery, and bread, and the Americanized version adds fennel-seasoned sausage and a cream base. My riff on this recipe takes the best of both versions to make a rich, aromatic, and highly flavorful soup.

---

16 ounces cremini mushrooms, quartered

Up to 1 teaspoon red pepper flakes

¼ cup coconut aminos

1 medium yellow onion, diced

6 garlic cloves, minced

½ cup dry white wine

2 pounds baby red potatoes, quartered with skins

1 pound carrots, cut to match the size of the quartered potatoes

1 celery stalk, chopped into ¼-inch-thick pieces

5 fresh thyme sprigs or 1 tablespoon dried thyme, plus more to garnish

2 bay leaves

2 tablespoons nutritional yeast

8 cups low-sodium vegetable stock

4 cups chopped kale leaves

1 (14-ounce) can full-fat coconut milk

1 (15-ounce) can cannellini beans, drained

Freshly ground black pepper

---

1. Place the mushrooms in a large pot over medium-high heat. Cook for 5 minutes, stirring once, until the mushrooms are slightly browned. Sprinkle with red pepper flakes to taste, then continue to cook, stirring, for 1 minute. Add the coconut aminos and cook for 1 minute more.

2. Add the onion and garlic to the pot and cook for 3 minutes, stirring occasionally. The onion should be translucent and light golden but not fully browned. Add the white wine and cook for about 3 minutes, until the wine has evaporated.

3. Stir in the potatoes, carrots, celery, thyme, bay leaf, and nutritional yeast. Pour in the stock and bring it to a simmer while stirring. Cover the pot, reduce the heat to medium-low, and cook for 10 to 15 minutes, until the potato can be pierced easily with a fork.

4. Stir in the kale, then the coconut milk and beans. Remove the bay leaves before serving.

5. Garnish with sprigs of fresh thyme and a few cracks of black pepper.

Per Serving: Calories: 292; Fat: 11g; Saturated Fat: 10g; Cholesterol: 0mg; Carbohydrates: 40g; Fiber: 9g; Protein: 7g; Sodium: 272mg

Chickpea "Chicken" Soup

ESSENTIAL RECIPE, NUT-FREE, SOY-FREE, CROWD-PLEASER,
WHOLE-FOOD PLANT-BASED

SERVES: 8 | **PREP TIME:** 15 minutes, not including
cooking pasta | **COOK TIME:** 20 minutes

There is nothing more comforting than chicken soup. In this recipe, steeped nutritional yeast makes a flavorful, umami-rich stock that is the perfect base for vegetables, herbs, and spices. The best part? You can have a hot bowl on your table in around 30 minutes!

½ cup nutritional yeast

1 cup boiling water

1 yellow onion, diced

3 garlic cloves, pressed or minced

3 large carrots, diced

3 celery stalks, sliced (add the leaves too)

1 tablespoon Italian seasoning

1 tablespoon water

8 cups low-sodium vegetable stock

2 (15-ounce) cans low-sodium chickpeas, drained and rinsed

¼ cup chopped fresh parsley

Table salt

Freshly ground black pepper

1 (1-pound) box gluten-free rotini pasta, cooked (optional)

1. In a measuring cup, whisk together the nutritional yeast and boiling water. Set aside, leaving the mixture undisturbed for at least 5 minutes.

2. In a large stock pot over medium heat, combine the onion, garlic, carrots, celery, Italian seasoning, and water. Cook the mixture for 5 minutes to soften the onion and vegetables slightly. If the vegetables stick to the pot or begin to cook too rapidly, add a little water, 1 tablespoon at a time, as needed. Add the vegetable stock and bring it to a boil, then reduce the heat to low, cover the pot, and simmer for 12 to 15 minutes, until the vegetables are tender.

3. Strain the nutritional yeast in a fine-mesh strainer set over a measuring cup or bowl. Pour the strained liquid into the stock pot. Save the remaining nutritional yeast sediment for other dishes that use nutritional yeast.

4. Stir the chickpeas and parsley into the soup, taste, and season with salt and pepper as needed.

5. Portion the cooked pasta into individual bowls, and pour the soup over the noodles to serve.

INGREDIENT SMARTS: Unlike its glutinous counterparts, gluten-free pasta does not hold up to long periods of time in hot water. The best method for serving gluten-free pasta in a soup is to add it directly to the bowls for serving.

Per Serving: Calories: 120; Fat: 2g; Saturated Fat: 0g; Cholesterol: 0mg; Carbohydrates: 20g; Fiber: 5g; Protein: 9g; Sodium: 166mg

Roasted Butternut Squash Soup

NUT-FREE, SOY-FREE, WHOLE-FOOD PLANT-BASED

SERVES: 8 | **PREP TIME:** 20 minutes | **COOK TIME:** 45 minutes

Roasting the butternut squash gives the soup a caramelly flavor, making it perfect for a cozy dinner. Top with a variety of garnishes: crisped tempeh, vegan yogurt or sour cream, a dash of chia seeds, or a sprinkle of pepitas.

- 4 medium carrots, chopped
- 1 large sweet potato, peeled and chopped
- 1 medium butternut squash, peeled, pulp removed, and cut into ½-inch cubes
- 1 medium yellow onion, chopped
- 3 garlic cloves, minced
- 1 tablespoon chili powder
- 1 teaspoon chipotle chile powder
- ½ teaspoon ground cinnamon
- 4 cups low-sodium vegetable stock
- 1 (14-ounce) can full-fat coconut milk

---

1. Preheat the oven to 425°F. Line a rimmed baking sheet with parchment.

2. Place the carrots, sweet potato, and butternut squash on the prepared baking sheet in a single layer. Roast for 20 minutes, flipping halfway. The squash should be tender and just starting to brown around the edges.

3. In a large pot over medium-high heat, combine the onion and garlic. Cook for 5 minutes, stirring, or until the onion is starting to brown. If the onion is cooking too quickly, add a little water (1 tablespoon at a time). Add both chili powders, cinnamon, and vegetable stock. Bring to a boil, reduce the heat to medium-high, and cook, uncovered, for 20 minutes.

4. Stir in the coconut milk and roasted vegetables, and use an immersion or upright blender to puree the soup until smooth. If using an upright blender, make sure to carefully follow the manufacturer's instructions for hot liquids. Serve hot.

Per Serving: Calories: 182; Fat: 11g; Saturated Fat: 9g; Cholesterol: 0mg; Carbohydrates: 22g; Fiber: 4g; Protein: 3g; Sodium: 70mg

Caribbean-Inspired Sweet Potato Soup

NUT-FREE, SOY-FREE, WHOLE-FOOD PLANT-BASED

SERVES: 4 | **PREP TIME:** 20 minutes | **COOK TIME:** 30 minutes

Traditionally called "callaloo," this Caribbean-inspired dish is the national dish of many of the region's countries, specifically Trinidad and Tobago. Authentic callaloo soup uses callaloo leaves, but I use easier-to-find spinach or kale instead.

---

2 tablespoons avocado oil (or ¼ cup water)

1 medium yellow onion, diced

1 red bell pepper, diced

4 garlic cloves, chopped

1 scotch bonnet or habanero chile, diced (optional)

2 cups cubed sweet potato

3 cups fresh or frozen okra, stemmed and chopped

2 tablespoons paprika

2 tablespoons dried thyme

2 cups full-fat coconut milk

2 cups low-sodium vegetable stock

1 to 2 cups water

5 cups chopped kale or spinach leaves

1 (14-ounce) can pumpkin puree

1 (14-ounce) can black-eyed peas, drained and rinsed

Table salt

Freshly ground black pepper

---

1. Heat the oil in a large pot over medium-high heat, add the onion, and cook for 5 minutes, stirring occasionally, until the onion is soft. Stir in the bell pepper, garlic, and chile (if desired), and cook for 3 minutes, until the bell pepper has softened. Add the sweet potato, okra, paprika, and thyme. Stir and cook for 2 minutes.

2. Stir in the coconut milk, stock, 1 to 2 cups of water, and kale or spinach. Bring to a boil, cover the pot, reduce the heat to medium, and cook for 20 minutes, until the sweet potato is tender.

3. Stir in the pumpkin and black-eyed peas until hot and season with salt and pepper.

Per Serving: Calories: 531; Fat: 33g; Saturated Fat: 23g; Cholesterol: 0mg; Carbohydrates: 55g; Fiber: 16g; Protein: 14g; Sodium: 114mg

Vegetables, Grains, and Sides

< Baked Miso
Sweet Potatoes,
page **104**

Sweet Corn Pudding

NUT-FREE, SOY-FREE

SERVES: 8 | **PREP TIME:** 10 minutes | **COOK TIME:** 45 minutes

This creamy corn casserole is a staple in the South. It's quick and easy and can be made both sweet or savory—enjoy it with a holiday dinner or as a weeknight meal. The sugar added to the recipe helps give structure to the overall dish, but it can be omitted if you prefer.

Nonstick cooking spray

1 (12-ounce) container firm silken tofu

¼ cup sugar

¼ cup vegan butter, melted

½ cup unsweetened gluten-free nondairy milk, homemade (page 218) or store-bought

½ teaspoon pure vanilla extract

1 (15-ounce) can cream-style corn

1 (15-ounce) can whole kernel corn, drained

½ cup 1:1 all-purpose gluten-free flour, homemade (page 206) or store-bought

¼ cup cornmeal

Dash ground nutmeg

2 teaspoons baking powder

1. Preheat the oven to 400°F. Spray a 9-by-13-inch baking dish with cooking spray. Set aside.

2. In a large bowl, whisk together the tofu and sugar, then mix in the melted butter, milk, and vanilla. Fold in the cream-style corn and whole kernel corn. Fold in the flour, cornmeal, nutmeg, and baking powder until no dry spots remain.

3. Pour the mixture into the prepared baking dish and use a spatula to level the top.

4. Bake for 40 to 50 minutes or until the top is lightly browned and the center is set and does not jiggle when you move the pan.

CHANGE IT UP: You can turn this into a Tex-Mex dish by omitting the vanilla, adding 1 (4-ounce) can diced chiles, and topping with vegan cheddar cheese.

Per Serving: Calories: 226; Fat: 9g; Saturated Fat: 1g; Cholesterol: 0mg; Carbohydrates: 35g; Fiber: 3g; Protein: 6g; Sodium: 97mg

Brussels Sprout Slaw

ESSENTIAL RECIPE, SOY-FREE, 30 MINUTES, CROWD-PLEASER

SERVES: 8 | **PREP TIME:** 20 minutes, not including dressing prep

Often, people make slaw just to have some kind of side dish on the table, but it's typically bland and sits ignored. This slaw uses a cruciferous cousin to cabbage, Brussels sprouts, and trust me, it will be the first dish on the table to disappear. Plus, it can be used as a crunchy topping for a burger or wrap.

1½ pounds Brussels sprouts, shredded (see Ingredient Smarts tip)

1 Granny Smith apple, cored and chopped

1 cup thinly sliced red onion

⅔ cup reduced sugar dried cranberries or raisins

½ cup chopped walnuts

¾ cup Basic Vinaigrette (page 223)

In a large salad bowl, combine the Brussels sprouts, apple, onion, dried cranberries, and walnuts, then toss with the dressing and serve.

INGREDIENT SMARTS: You can shred Brussels sprouts using the large holes on a box grater, a sharp knife, or the shredding disc in a food processor. Also, you can purchase pre-shredded Brussels sprouts in most grocery stores.

Per Serving: Calories: 125; Fat: 7g; Saturated Fat: 1g; Cholesterol: 0mg; Carbohydrates: 15g; Fiber: 5g; Protein: 4g; Sodium: 223mg

Pineapple-Cauliflower Rice

NUT-FREE, SOY-FREE, 30 MINUTES

SERVES: 4 | **PREP TIME:** 15 minutes | **COOK TIME:** 12 minutes

Cauliflower is high in fiber and has more vitamin C than an orange, but people often dislike it because it can be a little boring on its own. Ironically, though, the blandness of this cruciferous vegetable is actually its greatest attribute: Since cauliflower doesn't have a strong flavor, it's like the chameleon of veggies. This recipe kicks up the flavor with pineapple and coconut aminos.

1 medium cauliflower head, cut into florets

1 teaspoon sesame oil

2 teaspoons extra-virgin olive oil

¾ cup diced yellow onion

2 garlic cloves, minced

2 cups mixed frozen veggies (including corn, peas, and carrots), thawed

¼ cup coconut aminos

½ teaspoon table salt

¼ teaspoon freshly ground black pepper

¼ teaspoon cayenne pepper

1 cup diced pineapple, drained if canned

2 tablespoons sliced scallions, green parts only

1. Place the cauliflower florets in a food processor and pulse just until the cauliflower pieces are the size of rice. (Avoid overprocessing; the cauliflower will quickly go from riced to mushy if you pulse it too many times.) Set the cauliflower rice aside.

2. Heat a large nonstick sauté pan over medium-low heat. Pour in the sesame oil and olive oil and let the oils heat for about 1 minute, until they start to shimmer. Add the diced onion and garlic to the pan and cook, stirring occasionally, until the onion is translucent but not browned, about 3 minutes.

3. Add the cauliflower, mixed veggies, coconut aminos, salt, pepper, and cayenne to the pan and cook for about 5 minutes, stirring, until the cauliflower is softened slightly. Fold in the diced pineapple and cook, stirring, for 2 minutes, until hot.

4. Top the dish with the sliced scallions and serve.

MAKE AHEAD: Prepare the riced cauliflower up to 3 days ahead, or even purchase it in the produce section of most grocery stores. Frozen riced cauliflower won't work for this recipe because it loses too much of its texture. If you don't have a food processor, use the largest hole on a box grater, or mash the raw cauliflower florets with a potato masher until they are broken up, then chop the rest.

Per Serving: Calories: 182; Fat: 4g; Saturated Fat: 1g; Cholesterol: 0mg; Carbohydrates: 33g; Fiber: 8g; Protein: 7g; Sodium: 625mg

Mediterranean Pasta Salad

NUT-FREE, SOY-FREE, 30 MINUTES, CROWD-PLEASER

SERVES: 8 | **PREP TIME:** 20 minutes | **COOK TIME:** 6 minutes

A pasta salad is a good side dish and a great lunch option. This Mediterranean-inspired pasta salad will sweep you away to the hills of Provence in under 30 minutes, and it gets even better as it sits. Feel free to swap some of the ingredients to use up what you have in your refrigerator.

10 to 12 ounces gluten-free farfalle pasta

1 (15-ounce) can chickpeas, drained and rinsed

1 English cucumber, chopped

1 pint cherry or grape tomatoes, halved

½ cup sliced pitted kalamata olives

1 tablespoon chopped fresh parsley

1 teaspoon Italian seasoning

½ medium red onion, thinly sliced

¾ cup Basic Vinaigrette, Italian variation (page 223)

1. In a large pot of salted water, cook the pasta to al dente according to the package instructions, about 6 minutes. Drain the pasta in a colander, then rinse it under cold running water for 20 to 30 seconds, until it is no longer hot. Transfer the pasta to a large mixing bowl.

2. Add the chickpeas, cucumber, tomatoes, olives, parsley, Italian seasoning, and onion to the mixing bowl, then drizzle the vinaigrette over top. Using salad tongs or a large spoon, gently fold the ingredients together. Serve immediately or refrigerate for up to 1 week.

Per Serving: Calories: 211; Fat: 4g; Saturated Fat: 0g; Cholesterol: 0mg; Carbohydrates: 40g; Fiber: 7g; Protein: 5g; Sodium: 327mg

Cheesy Dill Carrots

NUT-FREE, 30 MINUTES, CROWD-PLEASER, WHOLE-FOOD PLANT-BASED

SERVES: 4 | **PREP TIME:** 10 minutes | **COOK TIME:** 10 minutes

This simple, five-ingredient side dish is loaded with flavor, color, and nutrients. The contrast between the bright orange and the vibrant green makes it a show-stopper, whether you're serving it for a holiday meal or as a quick weeknight side.

1 pound carrots, halved or quartered lengthwise and cut into 2-inch pieces, or baby carrots

1 cup water, divided

2 tablespoons white or yellow miso paste

1 tablespoon nutritional yeast (see Ingredient Smarts tip)

½ teaspoon onion powder

1 teaspoon dried dill

1. Heat the carrots in a nonstick frying pan over medium-high heat. Pour in ¾ cup of water. Cover the pan and cook over medium-high heat for 5 minutes or until the carrots have softened and can be pierced with a fork.

2. In a measuring cup, mix the remaining ¼ cup of water, miso, nutritional yeast, and onion powder. Stir well so that there aren't clumps of miso. It should be a thick mixture.

3. Pour the cheesy sauce over the carrots and cook for 2 minutes, stirring, over medium-high heat. Sprinkle the dill on the cheesy carrots and serve.

INGREDIENT SMARTS: Nutritional yeast is added to this recipe to give it a cheesy flavor that is similar to Parmesan cheese. Paired with the white miso paste, which has a cheddar flavor, these minimally seasoned carrots have a lot of flavor.

Per Serving: Calories: 66; Fat: 1g; Saturated Fat: 0g; Cholesterol: 0mg; Carbohydrates: 14g; Fiber: 4g; Protein: 2g; Sodium: 395mg

Mashed Cauliflower and Rutabaga with Roasted Garlic

NUT-FREE, SOY-FREE, CROWD-PLEASER

SERVES: 4 | **PREP TIME:** 20 minutes | **COOK TIME:** 30 minutes, plus 30 minutes (optional) garlic roasting time

Potatoes make up a large part of vegan, gluten-free diets, but there are so many wonderful root veggies to try. This recipe combines underused rutabaga with cauliflower for a scrumptious variation on humdrum mashed potatoes.

---

3 tablespoons vegan butter or extra-virgin olive oil

4 garlic cloves, roasted and mashed (see Technique Tip)

1 small cauliflower head, finely chopped

2 medium rutabagas, peeled and finely diced

2 cups low-sodium vegetable stock

2 teaspoons kosher salt

½ teaspoon freshly ground black pepper

1 teaspoon dried thyme

1 teaspoon dried parsley

---

1. Melt the butter in a large pot over medium-high heat, then add the garlic and cook for 1 minute, until fragrant. Stir in the cauliflower, rutabagas, and vegetable stock. Bring the liquid to a boil, reduce the heat to medium, cover the pot, and cook for 25 to 30 minutes, until the rutabagas can be easily pierced with a knife.

2. Once the vegetables have softened, remove the pot from the heat, uncover, and allow the vegetables to cool for 5 minutes. Use a hand mixer, immersion blender, food processor, or potato masher to mash the vegetables until smooth. Stir in the salt, pepper, thyme, and parsley before serving.

TECHNIQUE TIP: Roasting garlic ahead of time is an easy way to save meal prep minutes. Peel the garlic cloves, wrap them in aluminum foil, and bake at 400°F for 30 minutes. Store roasted garlic cloves in the refrigerator until you're ready to use them.

Per Serving: Calories: 182; Fat: 11g; Saturated Fat: 1g; Cholesterol: 0mg; Carbohydrates: 21g; Fiber: 6g; Protein: 4g; Sodium: 916mg

"Parmesan" Roasted Parsnip Fries

SOY-FREE, CROWD-PLEASER

SERVES: 4 | **PREP TIME:** 15 minutes | **COOK TIME:** 25 minutes

No one is saying that French fries are not incredible, but sometimes the starchy spuds could use a break. Bring in the parsnips, a unique but excellent alternative. Parsnips have a distinct flavor that pairs well with the seasoning blend in this recipe, and, once baked, their texture is a little crunchier than their potato counterpart.

3 tablespoons nutritional yeast

3 tablespoons almond flour

1 teaspoon onion powder

2½ pounds parsnips, scrubbed clean, peeled, cut into roughly 3-by-½-inch strips

3 tablespoons extra-virgin olive oil

1 teaspoon table salt, plus more for seasoning

1 garlic clove, finely minced

Freshly ground black pepper

1. Preheat the oven to 450°F. In a small bowl, whisk together the nutritional yeast, almond flour, and onion powder. Set aside.

2. On a large rimmed baking sheet, mix the parsnips with the oil, ensuring that the parsnips are evenly coated. Sprinkle the salt over top.

3. Roast the parsnips for 10 minutes, flip them over, and then roast for 15 more minutes. Remove the baking sheet from the oven. Sprinkle half of the seasoning mix and the garlic over the parsnip fries, flip, and sprinkle the remaining seasoning on top. Season with more salt and black pepper to taste. Serve immediately.

INGREDIENT SMARTS: Parsnips look like white carrots and can be found in the produce section of most grocery stores. Some stores purchase parsnips that are coated in a layer of wax, and this wax should be peeled off before roasting.

Per Serving: Calories: 322; Fat: 12g; Saturated Fat: 2g; Cholesterol: 0mg; Carbohydrates: 52g; Fiber: 14g; Protein: 4g; Sodium: 511mg

Baked Miso Sweet Potatoes

NUT-FREE, CROWD-PLEASER

SERVES: 4 | **PREP TIME:** 15 minutes | **COOK TIME:** 30 minutes

Roasting sweet potatoes brings out their rich umami and caramel flavors. Combined with butter, miso, and caramelized onion smakes this a flavorful side dish or appetizer that pairs well with salad, soup, or even toasted bread.

1½ tablespoons vegan butter, melted

2 teaspoons white or yellow miso

½ teaspoon freshly ground black pepper

¼ teaspoon table salt

3 medium sweet potatoes (1½ pounds total), scrubbed and cut into 1-inch rounds

1 medium yellow onion, sliced

1 tablespoon water

1 tablespoon pure maple syrup

1 tablespoon apple cider vinegar

1 tablespoon chopped fresh rosemary or 1 teaspoon dried rosemary

---

1. Preheat the oven to 425°F. Line a large rimmed baking sheet with parchment paper.

2. In a large bowl, whisk together the melted butter, miso, pepper, and salt. Add the sweet potato slices and toss to coat. Place the coated sweet potato slices in a single layer on the prepared baking sheet, and brush them with the remaining butter and miso mixture. Roast the sweet potatoes for 30 minutes, flipping once halfway.

3. While the sweet potatoes are roasting, caramelize the onion. Heat a nonstick frying pan over medium heat, add the onion, and cook for 5 minutes without stirring. Add a tablespoon of water, stir the onion slices, and turn the heat to medium-low. Cook until the onion slices are golden brown but not burned, about 20 minutes. Turn off the heat as soon as the onion is caramelized.

4. In a small bowl, whisk together the maple syrup and vinegar. Once the potatoes are out of the oven, drizzle the maple sauce over the sweet potatoes, top with the onion, and sprinkle with rosemary. Serve warm.

Per Serving: Calories: 215; Fat: 5g; Saturated Fat: 1g; Cholesterol: 0mg; Carbohydrates: 41g; Fiber: 6g; Protein: 3g; Sodium: 349mg

Garlic Butter Rice with Kale and Mushrooms

NUT-FREE, SOY-FREE

SERVES: 4 | **PREP TIME:** 20 minutes | **COOK TIME:** 25 minutes

Jasmine rice is highly aromatic, and vegan butter enhances its sweet, nutty flavors. This simple yet bold side dish can moonlight as a main dish with a little added protein, such as tempeh or chickpeas.

4 tablespoons vegan butter

1 large shallot, sliced

4 garlic cloves, minced

2 cups jasmine rice, rinsed

4 cups low-sodium golden vegetable stock (see Ingredient Smarts tip)

1 teaspoon kosher salt

1 bunch kale, stemmed and chopped

8 ounces cremini mushrooms, sliced

¼ cup coconut aminos

1. Melt the butter in a large pot over medium-high heat, then add the sliced shallot and garlic. Cook for 2 to 3 minutes, until the shallot starts to look translucent. Stir in the rinsed jasmine rice and cook, stirring continuously, for 2 minutes.

2. Pour in the vegetable stock and salt, stir, and bring to a boil. Reduce the heat to medium-low, cover, and cook for 15 minutes. Stir the rice, place the kale on top in an even layer, then cover the pot and cook without stirring for 5 minutes. Fold in the kale, turn off heat, and let sit for 5 minutes before serving.

3. While the rice cooks, heat a large nonstick frying pan over medium-high heat and add the mushrooms in a single layer. Cook for 5 minutes without moving the mushrooms, then pour in the coconut aminos, flip the mushrooms, and cook for 5 additional minutes, until the edges of the mushrooms are browned. Spoon the mushrooms on top of the rice to serve.

INGREDIENT SMARTS: You'll find brown and golden vegetable stock in stores. The ingredients are very similar, but the color of the stock will affect the color of your dish.

Per Serving: Calories: 490; Fat: 12g; Saturated Fat: 2g; Cholesterol: 0mg; Carbohydrates: 84g; Fiber: 4g; Protein: 10g; Sodium: 577mg

Pumpkin and Sage Risotto

NUT-FREE, SOY-FREE

SERVES: 4 | **PREP TIME:** 10 minutes | **COOK TIME:** 40 minutes

This creamy specialty is brought to us via Northern Italy, but its reputation precedes it. Risotto is often considered too challenging to conquer. However, if you have the right type of rice (Arborio) and the right technique (low and slow), it's really not that difficult. This risotto makes a delicious side dish that is great for any season of the year.

---

6 cups low-sodium vegetable stock

1 cup water

2 tablespoons vegan butter

4 garlic cloves, minced

2 large shallots, minced

2 cups Arborio rice

1 cup dry white wine

1 (15-ounce) can pumpkin puree

¼ cup nutritional yeast, plus extra for garnish

2 tablespoons minced fresh sage, plus a few leaves for garnish

Table salt

Freshly ground black pepper

---

1. In a small pot over medium-low heat, heat the stock and water. Warming the liquid will help the risotto cook evenly.

2. In a large pot over medium-high heat, melt the butter, then add the garlic and shallots. Cook for 2 to 3 minutes, stirring. Add the rice and cook for 2 minutes, stirring constantly. The grains of rice should start to become translucent around the edges. Pour in the wine and cook until it is absorbed.

3. Reduce the heat under the risotto to medium-low, and slowly add the stock mixture in increments, stirring after each addition. Add 1 cup of the stock mixture, stir to combine, then cook for 5 minutes or until the liquid has been absorbed. Repeat with the remaining liquid, 1 cup at a time, until you have 1 cup of stock remaining in the pot. This incremental procedure will take up to 30 minutes total. You will know this step is complete when you can run your spatula through the rice and the risotto slowly fills in the gap.

4. Stir in the pumpkin puree, nutritional yeast, sage, and final cup of stock, stirring to combine and cooking until most of the liquid has been absorbed and the risotto is creamy. This entire cooking process can take between 30 to 40 minutes, but you don't need to stir the entire time.

5. Remove the pot from the heat, taste, and season with salt and pepper to taste. Garnish with a sprinkle of nutritional yeast and fresh sage leaves, if desired.

Per Serving: Calories: 485; Fat: 7g; Saturated Fat: 1g; Cholesterol: 0mg; Carbohydrates: 88g; Fiber: 6g; Protein: 8g; Sodium: 57mg

Amaranth and Walnut Pilaf

SOY-FREE, 30 MINUTES, WHOLE-FOOD PLANT-BASED

SERVES: 4 | **PREP TIME:** 5 minutes | **COOK TIME:** 25 minutes

Amaranth is an especially high-quality source of plant protein (and fiber) because it includes two essential amino acids, lysine and methionine, that are not found in most other grains. This recipe comes together as a porridge consistency and takes no more than 30 minutes to make.

---

1 large shallot, thinly sliced

2 garlic cloves, minced

1 cup dry amaranth

2½ cups low-sodium vegetable stock

½ cup chopped walnuts

Juice of 1 lime

Table salt

Freshly ground black pepper, for garnish

Chopped fresh parsley, for garnish

---

1. Combine the shallot and garlic in a small pot over medium-high heat. Stir and cook for 3 minutes to soften the shallot. Stir in the amaranth and vegetable stock and bring to a boil. Reduce the heat to medium-low, cover the pot, and cook for 20 minutes. The amaranth will have absorbed the stock, and the grains should be fluffy.

2. Stir in the chopped walnuts, lime juice, and salt to taste. Serve immediately, topped with freshly ground black pepper and parsley.

CHANGE IT UP: Adding red kidney beans gives you additional protein and fiber, and halved grape tomatoes also bulk up this dish nicely. You can also substitute pumpkin and sunflower seeds for the walnuts if you want to omit the nuts.

Per Serving: Calories: 281; Fat: 13g; Saturated Fat: 2g; Cholesterol: 0mg; Carbohydrates: 35g; Fiber: 4g; Protein: 9g; Sodium: 42mg

Hasselback Potatoes

NUT-FREE, SOY-FREE, CROWD-PLEASER

SERVES: 4 | **PREP TIME:** 20 minutes | **COOK TIME:** 1 hour

The recipe is a crowd-wowing presentation, and it can turn a weeknight dinner into something special. Don't be afraid to get creative with toppings, such as vegan butter and chives or Sunflower Seed Cheese Sauce (page 210), but even plain, the crisp edges and soft center of these potatoes are absolutely dreamy.

4 medium russet potatoes

2 tablespoons vegan butter, melted

1 teaspoon kosher salt

2 tablespoons chopped fresh chives

Freshly ground black pepper

1. Preheat the oven to 450°F.

2. Place 2 disposable chopsticks or thin wooden spoons parallel to each other on a clean kitchen towel so they don't slip or move. Place the raw potato in the center of the chopsticks so only the bottom of the potato touches the towel. Starting at one end, carefully cut downward through the potato, stopping when your knife hits the chopsticks. Keep cutting slits, ¼ inch apart, until you reach the other side of the potato. Repeat with the remaining potatoes. This method ensures that you cut most of the way through the potato while still leaving it connected, to get that iconic Hasselback potato look.

3. Place the potatoes in an 8-by-8-inch glass baking dish. Using a basting brush or spoon, spread the butter between the potato slices; sprinkle with salt.

4. Bake for 55 to 60 minutes, uncovered, until the center slices of the potatoes can be easily pierced with a fork. You can crisp up the skins even more by broiling the potatoes for 2 to 3 minutes.

5. Top with fresh chives and black pepper to serve.

CHANGE IT UP: You can use any oil for this recipe in place of butter, but in order for the potatoes to have their distinct pieces, they need to have oil between each piece.

Per Serving: Calories: 219; Fat: 6g; Saturated Fat: 1g; Cholesterol: 0mg; Carbohydrates: 39g; Fiber: 3g; Protein: 5g; Sodium: 420mg

Roasted Carrots and Fennel

NUT-FREE, SOY-FREE, WHOLE-FOOD PLANT-BASED

SERVES: 4 | **PREP TIME:** 15 minutes | **COOK TIME:** 50 minutes

The natural sweetness of carrots pairs well with the distinct flavor and aroma of fresh fennel. This roasted side dish goes well with any special-occasion recipe, such as Veggie Pot Pie (page 158), Soy Curl–Stuffed Squash (page 173), and Zucchini Lasagna Pockets (page 168).

1½ pounds carrots, halved lengthwise and cut into 2-inch pieces

1 medium fennel bulb, cut into ½-inch chunks

2 tablespoons extra-virgin olive oil

1 teaspoon kosher salt

1 lemon, thinly sliced

1 tablespoon chopped fresh basil, oregano, or fennel fronds for garnish (optional)

---

1. Preheat the oven to 375°F. Line a large rimmed baking sheet with parchment paper and set aside.

2. In a large bowl, toss the carrots, fennel, and oil. Spread the vegetables on the prepared baking sheet, sprinkle with the salt, and place the slices of lemon over the vegetables.

3. Roast for 40 to 50 minutes without stirring, until the vegetables are tender and can be easily pierced with a fork. Discard the roasted lemon or serve it with the vegetables. Top with optional fresh herbs and enjoy.

INGREDIENT SMARTS: Fresh fennel, a vitamin C-heavy, slightly licorice-flavored ingredient, can be found in the refrigerated produce section of the grocery store. Save the leafy green tops to make vegetable stock, or use them as a garnish.

Per Serving: Calories: 148; Fat: 7g; Saturated Fat: 1g; Cholesterol: 0mg; Carbohydrates: 21g; Fiber: 7g; Protein: 2g; Sodium: 512mg

Wild Rice with Broccoli and Almonds

NUT-FREE, SOY-FREE, WHOLE-FOOD PLANT-BASED

SERVES: 4 | **PREP TIME:** 15 minutes | **COOK TIME:** 40 minutes

Wild rice is technically not rice because it comes from a type of grass. It's a great source of nutrients, including protein, fiber, and minerals like phosphorus and magnesium. The firm texture of the cooked wild rice in this recipe goes well with the steamed broccoli and blanched almonds.

2 garlic cloves, minced

4 cups water or low-sodium vegetable stock

1 cup wild rice

2 tablespoons chopped fresh thyme or dill

½ pound broccoli crowns, broken into small florets

¼ cup blanched slivered almonds

Freshly ground black pepper, for garnish

Chopped fresh parsley, for garnish

1. In a medium saucepan or pot, cook the garlic over medium-high heat for 30 seconds. Pour in the water and bring to a boil. Stir in the wild rice, reduce to a simmer over low heat, cover, and cook for 35 minutes.

2. Stir the rice to fluff it, top with the thyme or dill, then top with the broccoli florets. Cover the pot and continue to cook for an additional 5 minutes to steam the broccoli. Top with the blanched almonds and fold the mixture together, being careful not to break apart the broccoli.

3. Serve warm and top with freshly ground pepper and parsley to garnish.

CHANGE IT UP: If you want your rice dish to have a subtly different flavor and texture, you can substitute ¼ cup of brown rice for ¼ cup of the wild rice.

Per Serving: Calories: 205; Fat: 4g; Saturated Fat: 0g; Cholesterol: 0mg; Carbohydrates: 36g; Fiber: 5g; Protein: 9g; Sodium: 22mg

Roasted Cauliflower Wedges

NUT-FREE, SOY-FREE, CROWD-PLEASER

SERVES: 4 | **PREP TIME:** 15 minutes | **COOK TIME:** 30 minutes

These cauliflower wedges are a simple, colorful way to elevate your meal. The cauliflower is cut into large pieces and tossed in turmeric and other spices to make a vibrant yellow side dish. You can serve these wedges with a variety of toppings, but a simple drizzle of balsamic reduction and pomegranate seeds makes for an aesthetically pleasing, not to mention delicious, side.

---

1 large cauliflower head

1 teaspoon ground turmeric

½ teaspoon ground cumin

¼ teaspoon cayenne pepper (optional)

2 tablespoons extra-virgin olive oil

1 tablespoon balsamic reduction

¼ cup pomegranate seeds

---

1. Preheat the oven to 425°F. Line a large rimmed baking sheet with parchment paper.

2. Remove the leaves and trim the stem from the cauliflower head. Cut the cauliflower into eight wedges, cutting through from the bottom to the crown of the cauliflower, and set the wedges on the prepared baking sheet.

3. In a small metal or glass bowl, mix together the turmeric, cumin, cayenne, and oil. Be careful to not get the turmeric on your clothes because it will stain. Brush the cauliflower wedges with the seasoned oil, or carefully toss the cauliflower in the oil mixture.

4. Roast the cauliflower for 30 minutes, until tender. Once plated, drizzle the wedges with the balsamic reduction and sprinkle the pomegranate seeds over top. Serve warm.

CHANGE IT UP: You can replace the oil with an equal amount of water in this recipe to make it a whole food, plant-based dish. Swapping the oil for water will change the browning of your wedges, making them a little drier on the edges, but the dish will still be colorful and delicious.

Per Serving: Calories: 128; Fat: 8g; Saturated Fat: 1g; Cholesterol: 0mg; Carbohydrates: 14g; Fiber: 5g; Protein: 4g; Sodium: 65mg

Roasted Beets with Orange Sauce and Olives

NUT-FREE, SOY-FREE

SERVES: 4 | **PREP TIME:** 20 minutes | **COOK TIME:** 1 hour

Beets are an easy way to add color to your dinner table—plus, they are a great source of many nutrients, including nitrates, which lower blood pressure. The beets in this recipe are roasted with an orange glaze to add a pleasant zing to the earthy, sweet root vegetable, while olives add a savory pop of flavor.

Nonstick cooking spray

Zest and juice of
1 navel orange

1 tablespoon pure
maple syrup

1½ teaspoons
balsamic vinegar

1 teaspoon Dijon mustard

½ teaspoon extra-virgin
olive oil

3 medium red beets, peeled
and cut into 8 pieces each

Freshly ground
black pepper

¼ cup chopped
kalamata olives

---

1. Preheat the oven to 350°F. Spray a 9-by-13-inch glass baking dish with cooking spray. Set aside.

2. In a large saucepan, whisk together the orange juice and zest, maple syrup, balsamic vinegar, mustard, and oil. Heat over medium-high heat while whisking until the sauce starts to bubble. Remove from the heat.

3. Add the beets to the saucepan, toss them with the orange glaze, and then transfer them to the prepared baking dish, spreading them out in a single layer. Cover the dish with foil and roast for 60 minutes, until the beets are tender and can be easily pierced with a fork. Serve warm with black pepper and the olives.

MAKE AHEAD: This dish can be stored for a couple of days in the refrigerator prior to serving. You can reheat these beets for a warm dish or serve them cold with fresh arugula, spring greens, or spinach for a salad option.

Per Serving: Calories: 66; Fat: 2g; Saturated Fat: 0g; Cholesterol: 0mg; Carbohydrates: 12g; Fiber: 2g; Protein: 1g; Sodium: 125mg

Weeknight Main Dishes

< Black Bean–Quinoa
Burgers, page **116**

Black Bean–Quinoa Burgers

ESSENTIAL RECIPE, NUT-FREE, SOY-FREE, CROWD-PLEASER

MAKES: 6 burgers | **PREP TIME:** 20 minutes, plus 30 minutes
chilling time | **COOK TIME:** 15 minutes, not including cooking quinoa

Black bean burgers are a staple for any vegan kitchen, but it is often challenging to find a sturdy gluten-free recipe. This recipe uses cooked quinoa for texture, chickpea flour to help it stay together, and lots of spices for flavor. Enjoy the burgers on gluten-free Burger Buns (page 202) topped with vegan provolone and some Sun-Dried-Tomato Ketchup (page 216).

½ cup dried quinoa, rinsed, or 1 cup cooked quinoa

1 cup plus 2 tablespoons water, divided

2 tablespoons extra-virgin olive oil, divided

2 garlic cloves, minced

1 medium yellow onion, diced

1 red bell pepper, seeded and diced

¼ cup chopped fresh cilantro

1 (32-ounce) can black beans, drained and rinsed

2 tablespoons chickpea flour

1 tablespoon liquid smoke

2 teaspoons smoked paprika

2 teaspoons ground cumin

2 teaspoons table salt

1 teaspoon red pepper flakes (optional)

---

1. If using dry quinoa, in a small pot, bring 1 cup of water to a boil. Add the quinoa, stir, cover, and cook over medium-low heat for 15 minutes. Set aside. (This step could also be done a day in advance and the cooked quinoa stored in the refrigerator.)

2. In a nonstick skillet, heat 1 tablespoon of oil over medium-high heat and sauté the garlic, onion, and bell pepper for 3 minutes, stirring. Turn off the heat, stir in the cilantro, and set aside to cool for 5 to 10 minutes.

3. Scoop the cooked veggies into a food processor and pulse with the beans and quinoa until combined. Transfer the mixture to a large bowl and mix in the chickpea flour, liquid smoke, paprika, cumin, salt, and red pepper flakes, if using. If the mixture looks dry, add the remaining 2 tablespoons of water.

4. Divide the mixture into 6 parts and shape into ½-inch patties. Line a large rimmed baking sheet with parchment paper, place the patties on the prepared baking sheet, and refrigerate, uncovered, for 30 minutes. If you want to make the patties ahead, you can cover them at this stage and either refrigerate for the next day or freeze for future use.

5. In a skillet over medium heat, add the remaining tablespoon of oil, and carefully place the burgers into the pan. Cook for 3 to 5 minutes on each side, until the tops are golden brown and the outside of the patties looks dry.

MAKE AHEAD: These black bean burgers can be made as a large batch and then frozen for future use. The best way to freeze them is to put them on a parchment-lined baking sheet, cover with aluminum foil or plastic wrap, and freeze on the baking sheet before transferring to a bag or wrapping in foil. It is also helpful to have a piece of parchment paper between the patties when storing so that it is easier to separate them while frozen.

Per Serving (1 burger): Calories: 233; Fat: 6g; Saturated Fat: 1g; Cholesterol: 0mg; Carbohydrates: 35g; Fiber: 10g; Protein: 11g; Sodium: 672mg

Lentil Burgers

NUT-FREE, SOY-FREE, CROWD-PLEASER

MAKES: 6 burgers | **PREP TIME:** 20 minutes, plus 30 minutes chilling time | **COOK TIME:** 50 minutes

Cooked lentils and caramelized onions are mashed and pressed into patties that are seasoned with cumin and other common spices. This is a great weeknight meal option, because you can make the lentils or even the whole burgers ahead of time. The burgers also freeze well.

½ cup green or brown dried lentils, rinsed and picked over

1½ cups water

1 medium white onion, chopped

1½ cups gluten-free oats

4 garlic cloves, minced

½ cup chopped celery

3 tablespoons coconut aminos

1 tablespoon paprika

1 teaspoon ground cumin

1 teaspoon ground coriander

2 teaspoons table salt

1 tablespoon Dijon mustard

Zest of ½ lemon

1 tablespoon tahini

1 tablespoon extra-virgin olive oil

1. Bring a small pot of water to a boil and stir in the lentils. Cover and cook over medium-low heat for 20 minutes. Drain the lentils and set aside. This step could also be done a day in advance; store the cooked lentils in an airtight container in the refrigerator.

2. While the lentils cook, sauté the onion in a small nonstick frying pan over medium-low heat for 20 minutes, stirring periodically and adding a little water every few minutes (1 tablespoon at a time) to prevent burning. Once the onion is golden and starting to brown, turn off the heat and set the pan aside.

3. In a blender or food processor, pulse the oats a few times until they reach the consistency of coarse flour

4. In a large mixing bowl, mix together the oat flour, cooked lentils, caramelized onions, garlic, and celery. Mash until fully combined.

5. Using a heavy spoon, mix in the aminos, paprika, cumin, coriander, salt, mustard, and lemon zest. When everything is fully combined, mix in the tahini. Cover and refrigerate for a minimum of 30 minutes.

6. In a large nonstick frying pan, heat the oil over medium heat.

7. Keep the burger mixture in the bowl, and use a knife to divide it into 6 equal parts. Using wet hands, shape each part into a ½-inch-thick patty, and carefully place the patties in the hot pan. Cook the patties for 4 to 5 minutes per side, until browned. Enjoy immediately.

MAKE AHEAD: If making these patties in advance, you can refrigerate the dough in the bowl overnight to be shaped the next day, or you can shape the patties and freeze them on a parchment-lined baking sheet. To reheat an already cooked patty, place it in a hot pan, with or without oil, and cook each side for 1 to 2 minutes.

Per Serving (1 burger): Calories: 238; Fat: 6g; Saturated Fat: 1g; Cholesterol: 0mg; Carbohydrates: 36g; Fiber: 7g; Protein: 11g; Sodium: 823mg

Sweet Potatoes with Quinoa-Walnut Filling

SOY-FREE, CROWD-PLEASER

SERVES: 4 | **PREP TIME:** 20 minutes | **COOK TIME:** 1 hour 10 minutes

This recipe is perfect for a busy weeknight because you can prepare the quinoa and sweet potato and chop the veggies ahead of time, making it a heat-and-eat meal. The flavors in this dish are built by combining a range of umami-rich ingredients and then brightening the filling with cilantro and a little citrus.

---

4 medium sweet potatoes, washed and dried

1 cup sun-dried tomatoes, not oil-packed

1 to 2 cups boiling water

½ cup dried quinoa, rinsed

1 cup raw walnuts

4 garlic cloves

1 tablespoon nutritional yeast

¼ cup chopped fresh cilantro

2 teaspoons ground cumin

2 teaspoons paprika

1 teaspoon chili powder

Juice of 1 lime

Juice of 1 small orange

Table salt

1 tablespoon avocado oil

1 medium red onion, finely diced

1 yellow bell pepper, seeded and finely diced

Avocado slices, for serving (optional)

Hot sauce, for topping (optional)

Vegan sour cream, for topping (optional)

---

1. If baking the sweet potatoes, preheat the oven to 425°F. Prick the skin with a fork or knife, place the sweet potatoes on a large rimmed baking sheet, and bake for 45 to 50 minutes. If microwaving, prick the skin and microwave on high for 5 minutes and adjust the time if microwaving more than one. This step can be done in advance.

2. In a glass or metal bowl, measure out the sun-dried tomatoes. Pour enough boiling water over top to cover the tomatoes by 2 inches and set aside. Drain after 20 minutes.

3. In a small pot, bring more water to a boil, pour in the quinoa, stir, cover, and cook over medium-low heat for 15 minutes. Set aside. This step could also be done a day in advance; store the cooked quinoa in the refrigerator.

4. In a food processor, pulse the walnuts until coarsely ground.

5. Add the quinoa, garlic, sun-dried tomatoes, nutritional yeast, cilantro, cumin, paprika, chili powder, and lime and orange juices to the food processor. Season with salt to taste, and pulse until combined.

6. In a large nonstick skillet, warm the oil over medium-low heat and sauté the onion and pepper for 2 minutes, while stirring. Add the quinoa mixture to the pan and cook until slightly browned, about 5 minutes.

7. Serve immediately on the prepared sweet potatoes. This loaded potato is perfect to top with some creamy avocado slices or even a drizzle of hot sauce or vegan sour cream.

Per Serving: Calories: 498; Fat: 25g; Saturated Fat: 3g; Cholesterol: 0mg; Carbohydrates: 63g; Fiber: 11g; Protein: 13g; Sodium: 170mg

Buffalo Chickpea Sliders

NUT-FREE, SOY-FREE, CROWD-PLEASER

MAKES: 8 sliders | **PREP TIME:** 20 minutes, plus 1 hour chilling time | **COOK TIME:** 20 minutes

Get ready for game day! These crispy patties have a gluten-free panko coating and get some zip from Buffalo Sauce (page 221). Serve them on mini gluten-free burger buns or with seared zucchini coins.

1 (15-ounce) can chickpeas, drained and rinsed

¼ cup brown rice flour

¼ cup Buffalo Sauce (page 221)

¼ cup chopped fresh cilantro

2 teaspoons garlic powder

1 teaspoon smoked paprika

1 teaspoon ground cumin

½ teaspoon freshly ground black pepper

1 teaspoon table salt

1 cup gluten-free panko breadcrumbs

8 slider-size Burger Buns (page 202; form the dough into half-size buns)

1. In a large bowl, mix all of the ingredients through the salt. Once the chickpeas are coated, mash using a potato masher or heavy spoon. Transfer the bowl to the fridge and refrigerate for 1 hour.

2. Preheat the oven to 375°F. Line a large rimmed baking sheet with parchment paper. Measure the breadcrumbs into a small bowl. Set aside.

3. Divide the burger mixture into 8 equal parts. Using wet hands, shape each part into a 1-inch-thick patty and roll with breadcrumbs. Place the coated patties on the baking sheet. Bake for 20 minutes, flipping after 10 minutes, until the patties are lightly browned.

4. Serve on slider-size Burger Buns.

Per Serving (2 sliders): Calories: 282; Fat: 5g; Saturated Fat: 1g; Cholesterol: 1mg; Carbohydrates: 54g; Fiber: 2g; Protein: 5g; Sodium: 361mg

Hummus Pasta

NUT-FREE, SOY-FREE, 30 MINUTES, CROWD-PLEASER

SERVES: 4 | **PREP TIME:** 10 minutes | **COOK TIME:** 18 minutes

This recipe uses the natural creaminess of hummus as a sauce, plus unique umami flavors and a touch of lemon for brightness. This meal is high in fiber and protein, and it is very satisfying without feeling heavy.

---

1 pound gluten-free rotini, penne, or elbow pasta

1 tablespoon extra-virgin olive oil

3 cups small broccoli florets

4 garlic cloves, minced

1 cup sun-dried tomatoes in oil, drained and roughly chopped

½ cup pitted kalamata olives, chopped

1 cup full-fat coconut milk

1 tablespoon freshly squeezed lemon juice

1 teaspoon dried oregano

½ teaspoon dried basil

½ teaspoon kosher salt

1 cup plain hummus

2 tablespoons tahini

Freshly ground black pepper

---

1. Cook the pasta according to the package instructions, then drain and rinse it under cool running water. Make sure not to overcook gluten-free pasta, as it breaks down easily.

2. Heat the oil in a large nonstick frying pan over medium-high heat. Add the broccoli and sauté for 3 minutes, flipping and turning occasionally. Add the garlic, sun-dried tomatoes, and olives to the pan and cook for 5 minutes, stirring occasionally.

3. Pour in the coconut milk, lemon juice, oregano, basil, and salt and bring to a low simmer. Remove the pan from the heat and mix in the hummus and tahini until the sauce is smooth and everything is fully incorporated. Add black pepper to taste. Pour the cooked pasta into the pan, mix gently, and serve immediately.

Per Serving: Calories: 823; Fat: 32g; Saturated Fat: 14g; Cholesterol: 0mg; Carbohydrates: 114g; Fiber: 11g; Protein: 24g; Sodium: 682mg

The Best Vegan Chili

ESSENTIAL RECIPE, NUT-FREE, SOY-FREE, CROWD-PLEASER

SERVES: 12 | **PREP TIME:** 20 minutes, plus overnight
bean soaking | **COOK TIME:** 45 to 55 minutes

This is, hands down, the best vegan chili, thanks to a couple of unusual ingredients such as molasses, amaranth, and dried shiitake mushrooms. You'll enjoy both a meaty texture and, with the variety of umami-rich ingredients, a complex flavor, even though you're using mostly common ingredients. If you don't have a pressure cooker, you can use a slow cooker or even cook it on the stove with some modifications. See the Technique Tip for details.

½ pound dried black beans, or 2 (15-ounce) cans black beans, drained and rinsed

½ pound dried great northern beans, or 2 (15-ounce) cans great northern beans, drained and rinsed

3 medium yellow onions, chopped

6 garlic cloves, minced

1 (4-ounce) can tomato paste

3 tablespoons avocado oil

1 tablespoon ground cumin

1 tablespoon dried oregano

1 tablespoon dried parsley

2 tablespoons chili powder

1 tablespoon ancho chile powder

¼ cup coconut aminos

8 cups low-sodium vegetable stock

1 tablespoon molasses

3 medium carrots, diced

¼ cup dried shiitake mushrooms, coarsely chopped

½ cup dried whole-grain amaranth

¼ cup minced fresh cilantro

1 (28-ounce) can tomato puree

---

1. If using dried beans, place them in a large bowl, pour in enough cool water to cover them by 2 inches, and let them soak overnight. Drain well. (If you're using canned beans, you'll add those in at the end before serving.)

2. Set your pressure cooker to sauté and cook the onion and garlic for about 3 minutes, using a tablespoon of water at a time until it is just beginning to brown. This water sautéing method is used to eliminate oil when it is not necessary.

3. Mix in the tomato paste and oil and cook for 1 to 2 minutes, stirring. Add the cumin, oregano, parsley, and both chili powders; mix to combine.

4. Add the soaked dried beans (if using), coconut aminos. vegetable stock, molasses, carrots, and mushrooms. Close the pressure cooker and set the vent to seal. Cook for 15 minutes on high pressure, then let the pressure release naturally, which will take anywhere from 15 to 30 minutes.

5. Stir in the amaranth and cilantro. Add the tomato puree, but don't stir it in; let it sit on the top of the chili mixture. Set the pressure cooker to cook for 5 minutes on high pressure, then manually release the steam. If using canned beans, add them now. Serve the chili warm with vegan sour cream and additional chopped cilantro, if desired.

TECHNIQUE TIP: If you don't have an electric pressure cooker, simply cook the dried beans ahead of time or use canned beans, and follow the same steps using a large soup pot or Dutch oven. You can also use a slow cooker: Sauté the onions and garlic, then stir in all the ingredients and cook on Low for at least 8 hours.

Per Serving: Calories: 254; Fat: 5g; Saturated Fat: 1g; Cholesterol: 0mg; Carbohydrates: 44g; Fiber: 11g; Protein: 12g; Sodium: 568mg

Soba Noodle Ramen Bowls

NUT-FREE, SOY-FREE, CROWD-PLEASER

SERVES: 4 | **PREP TIME:** 15 minutes | **COOK TIME:** 18 minutes

Soba noodles, made out of buckwheat, are used to make this easily customizable ramen bowl, a perfect crowd-pleaser that can be tailored to any taste. The base of the noodle bowl is an easy-to-make broth that you can load up with fresh veggies, tofu, and any other items you choose to throw in.

FOR THE BASE

4 cups water

8 ounces dried soba noodles

2 teaspoons sesame oil

2 teaspoons chili oil (or use neutral oil and ½ teaspoon red pepper flakes)

4 garlic cloves, minced

½ cup coconut aminos

6 dried shiitake mushrooms

2 teaspoons grated fresh ginger

2 tablespoons rice vinegar

2 tablespoons nutritional yeast

8 cups low-sodium vegetable stock

FOR THE RAMEN BOWLS

1 carrot, grated and peeled

1 fresh shiitake mushroom, thinly sliced

2 tablespoons sliced scallions, green parts only

6 snow peas

¾ cup firm silken tofu

1 tablespoon coconut aminos

1 teaspoon chopped fresh cilantro

1 teaspoon gluten-free sriracha sauce

1. To make the base: In a medium stock pot, bring the water to a boil. Add the soba noodles and cook for 6 minutes. Drain the noodles in a colander and rinse them under cold running water to remove any starch. Leave the noodles in the colander.

2. Rinse out the stock pot, return it to the stove over medium heat, and add the sesame and chili oils and garlic. Sauté the garlic for 30 seconds, just until fragrant, then immediately add the coconut aminos, mushrooms, ginger, vinegar, nutritional yeast, and vegetable stock; simmer uncovered for 10 minutes.

3. To make the ramen bowls: While the broth simmers, build your ramen bowls by dividing the cooked and rinsed soba noodles among 4 individual soup bowls. I like to add some of the toppings in the bottom of the bowl so they cook a little in the hot broth, then add more to the top so they stay crunchy and fresh. Ladle the broth into the individual bowls, pouring it through a fine-mesh strainer, and serve.

Per Serving: Calories: 310; Fat: 7g; Saturated Fat: 1g; Cholesterol: 0mg; Carbohydrates: 53g; Fiber: 2g; Protein: 15g; Sodium: 1,173mg

BBQ Soy Curl Hoagies

NUT-FREE, 30 MINUTES, CROWD-PLEASER

SERVES: 4 | **PREP TIME:** 10 minutes | **COOK TIME:** 6 minutes

Soy curls are good to have on hand because they don't require cooking, only a soak in warm water. They can be seasoned in any way you can imagine, they are high in protein, and they have a meaty texture that doesn't come from heavy processing. For this recipe, you can use BBQ Sauce (page 207) and a modified version of the Burger Buns (page 202), or feel free to use store-bought versions.

2 cups dried soy curls

3 to 4 cups warm water

1 tablespoon smoked paprika

1 teaspoon garlic powder

1 teaspoon onion powder

2 tablespoons coconut aminos

1 tablespoon avocado oil

1 medium yellow onion, sliced thin

1 to 2 cups gluten-free and vegan BBQ sauce, homemade (page 207) or store-bought

4 hoagie-size gluten-free rolls, homemade (see Ingredient Smarts tip) or store-bought

1. In a large bowl, combine the soy curls and warm water, using enough to cover them. Let them sit for 8 minutes to soak. Drain the water by gently pressing on the soaked soy curls with your hand and then tilting the bowl over the sink to pour out the water.

2. Mix in the paprika, garlic powder, onion powder, and coconut aminos with the soaked soy curls.

3. In a large nonstick frying pan, heat the oil over high heat. Add the onion and cook for 1 minute. Add the seasoned soy curls and toss to coat with oil and mix with the onion. Cook for 5 minutes or until the soy curls start to blacken around the edges. Remove from the heat.

4. Stir in 1 cup of BBQ sauce and add more, based on preference. Divide the soy curls among the 4 buns. Enjoy as is, or add vegan mozzarella, sliced dill pickles, or sauerkraut.

INGREDIENT SMARTS: The most common brand of soy curls is Butler Foods; they can be found in some grocery stores, but it is easier to order bags online. To make hoagie buns, use the burger bun recipe on page 202, but double the size of the dough balls and form them into long rather than round shapes before baking.

Per Serving: Calories: 665; Fat: 11g; Saturated Fat: 2g; Cholesterol: 1mg; Carbohydrates: 112g; Fiber: 4g; Protein: 34g; Sodium: 1,054mg

Corn Tortilla Enchilada Lasagna

NUT-FREE, SOY-FREE, CROWD-PLEASER

SERVES: 8 | **PREP TIME:** 30 minutes, not including enchilada sauce prep | **COOK TIME:** 30 minutes

Enchiladas might seem too fussy for busy weeknights, but since this recipe skips the rolling step to save time, it becomes an almost effortless meal. To save even more time, make this casserole ahead and refrigerate it for up to two days. Get creative with the veggies in the layers if you're feeling adventurous.

Nonstick cooking spray

18 small corn tortillas

1 tablespoon extra-virgin olive oil

8 ounces button mushrooms, chopped

1 medium yellow onion, chopped

4 garlic cloves, minced

1 cup frozen lima beans

2 cups roughly chopped spinach

1 tablespoon ground cumin

1 teaspoon dried oregano

1 (15-ounce) can vegan refried beans

1 (15-ounce) can black beans, not drained

2 cups Enchilada Sauce (page 214)

1 (14-ounce) can corn kernels, drained

1 cup shredded vegan cheddar cheese (such as Violife or Parmela)

---

1. Preheat the oven to 425°F.

2. Spray a 9-by-13-inch baking dish with cooking spray. Set aside. Cut 6 of the tortillas in half.

3. Heat the oil in a large nonstick pan over medium-high heat. Add the mushrooms, onion, and garlic, and sauté for 5 minutes. Stir in the lima beans, spinach, cumin, oregano, refried beans, and black beans. Mix well and cook, stirring, just until the spinach wilts and the lima beans are thawed.

4. Spread a couple spoonfuls of the enchilada sauce onto the bottom of the baking dish. Place 2 whole tortillas side by side in the center of the dish so they overlap slightly. Place a cut tortilla so that the flat edge faces the end of the dish, and repeat on the other side to make an even layer of tortillas across the bottom of the dish. Gently spread half of the bean mixture on top of the tortillas in an even layer. Top with half of the corn and 1 cup of enchilada sauce.

5. Repeat step 4 for a second layer. Top with the remaining enchilada sauce and the vegan cheddar cheese. Bake for 25 to 30 minutes. Let stand for 10 minutes prior to serving.

INGREDIENT SMARTS: Every brand of vegan cheese is slightly different in terms of how it melts and bakes. You can also omit the cheese or substitute it with Sunflower Seed Cheese Sauce (page 210).

Per Serving: Calories: 422; Fat: 12g; Saturated Fat: 3g; Cholesterol: 0mg; Carbohydrates: 66g; Fiber: 12g; Protein: 19g; Sodium: 638mg

Edamame Pesto Pasta

30 MINUTES, CROWD-PLEASER

SERVES: 6 | **PREP TIME:** 10 minutes | **COOK TIME:** 10 minutes

This highly flavorful, colorful, and protein-rich dish comes together in just minutes. The fresh basil and roasted garlic are key ingredients for this recipe's flavor and potent aroma. You can save yourself cooking and prep time by purchasing pre-roasted garlic, which is sold in the refrigerated section of most grocery stores near the fresh herbs.

¼ cup unsalted raw almonds

1 cup frozen shelled edamame, thawed

1 tablespoon roasted garlic paste (see Make Ahead tip), or 3 garlic cloves, minced

1 cup packed fresh basil leaves

1 cup packed spinach

1 tablespoon freshly squeezed lemon juice

1 teaspoon lemon zest

¼ cup nutritional yeast

Table salt

¼ cup extra-virgin olive oil

1 pound gluten-free pasta

---

1. In a large nonstick frying pan, toast the almonds over medium-low heat for about 3 minutes until they're lightly browned and fragrant, stirring often. Place them on a plate or baking sheet.

2. Heat the same frying pan over high heat; add the thawed edamame and roasted garlic and cook for 5 minutes, stirring occasionally, until the edamame are bright green with some golden spots. Remove the pan from the heat and let cool.

3. Using a food processor, chop the toasted almonds with a couple of pulses. Add the edamame and garlic, basil, and spinach, and blend until the mixture becomes a thick paste.

4. Add the lemon juice, zest, nutritional yeast, and salt to taste. Pulse to mix while slowly adding the oil.

5. Cook the gluten-free pasta according to the package instructions and make sure to rinse. Toss the cooked pasta with the pesto and serve as is, or add cooked carrots, tofu, tempeh, or toppings like red pepper flakes and capers.

MAKE AHEAD: To make your own garlic paste, peel garlic cloves, trim off the tough ends, and wrap the cloves in aluminum foil. Roast in a 350°F oven for 20 minutes or until tender. Once the cloves are cooked, they can be left whole or mashed into a paste before refrigerating or freezing.

Per Serving: Calories: 431; Fat: 15g; Saturated Fat: 2g; Cholesterol: 0mg; Carbohydrates: 66g; Fiber: 11g; Protein: 11g; Sodium: 179mg

TVP Meatball Subs

NUT-FREE, CROWD-PLEASER

MAKES: 14 TVP meatballs | **PREP TIME:** 20 minutes | **COOK TIME:** 20 minutes

Texturized vegetable protein, or TVP, is a must for any vegan kitchen because it is quick to prepare, high in protein, and neutral in flavor, allowing it to be seasoned however you'd like. This TVP meatball sub can be made in under an hour or prepped ahead for an even faster dinner. You can also use TVP in place of ground beef for a quick sloppy joe, in chili, or to add texture to gravy.

1 cup low-sodium vegetable stock

1 cup dry texturized vegetable protein (TVP)

1 tablespoon extra-virgin olive oil

4 garlic cloves, minced

¼ cup tomato paste

1 teaspoon dried oregano

1 teaspoon dried basil

1 teaspoon rosemary

½ teaspoon fennel seed (optional)

2 tablespoons coconut aminos

1 tablespoon liquid smoke

Table salt

1 tablespoon nutritional yeast

4 to 6 tablespoons rice flour

3 to 4 tablespoons avocado oil

4 gluten-free burger buns, homemade (page 202) or store-bought (optional)

2 cups marinara sauce, for serving (optional)

1. In a medium saucepan, bring the vegetable stock to a boil. Remove from the heat and mix in the TVP. Cover with a lid and set aside for 5 minutes.

2. In a large nonstick frying pan, heat the oil over medium-high heat and sauté the garlic for 1 minute while stirring. Add the tomato paste and continue to cook for 2 minutes, stirring. Mix in the hydrated TVP, oregano, basil, rosemary, fennel seeds (if using), coconut aminos, liquid smoke, and salt to taste. Cook for 3 minutes or until thick, stirring often. Remove from the heat and allow the mixture to cool enough to be handled.

3. Transfer the mixture to a large mixing bowl, mixing in nutritional yeast and 4 tablespoons rice flour. Add more rice flour if the mixture feels too wet to make an easy-to-handle dough.

4. Divide the meatball mixture into 14 equal parts, roll between your hands to form 1-inch balls, and place them on a parchment-lined baking sheet.

5. Using the same pan as earlier, wiped clean, pour 3 to 4 tablespoons of oil into the pan and heat over medium-high until the oil starts to shimmer. There should be enough oil in the pan to completely cover the bottom. Place the shaped balls into the hot oil and cook for 6 to 8 minutes, turning them periodically with a spatula or spoon.

6. Serve the meatballs warm on a gluten-free bun, tortilla, or coated with marinara sauce for a messier meal.

CHANGE IT UP: You can bake these "meatballs" at 375° F for 25 to 30 minutes if you prefer not to use additional oil.

Per Serving (2 meatballs): Calories: 198; Fat: 8g; Saturated Fat: 1g; Cholesterol: 0mg; Carbohydrates: 17g; Fiber: 6g; Protein: 15g; Sodium: 155mg

Tempeh Tacos

NUT-FREE, CROWD-PLEASER

SERVES: 6 | **PREP TIME:** 15 minutes, not including the cheese or enchilada sauce | **COOK TIME:** 20 minutes

You'll love this twist on traditional Mexican street fare. Nutty, protein- and fiber-rich tempeh is the star of this recipe. Paired with shiitake mushrooms and soaked sun-dried tomatoes, it makes a meaty taco base that gets served with a drizzle of cheese sauce and a little enchilada sauce or hot sauce.

---

1 tablespoon avocado oil

½ cup chopped yellow onion

1 cup diced sweet potato

¼ cup water

1 medium red bell pepper, seeded and diced

4 ounces (1 cup) shiitake mushroom, chopped

½ cup sun-dried tomatoes in oil, drained and chopped

1 tablespoon apple cider vinegar

8 ounces tempeh

1 tablespoon coconut aminos

1 tablespoon pure maple syrup

1 tablespoon All-Purpose Seasoning (page 220) or store-bought taco seasoning

Table salt

Freshly ground black pepper

6 gluten-free, vegan taco shells or tortillas

1 cup Enchilada Sauce (page 214), for topping

1 cup Sunflower Seed Cheese Sauce (page 210), for topping

Avocado slices, for topping

Cherry tomatoes, halved, for topping

Arugula, for topping

---

1. In a large nonstick frying pan, warm the oil over medium heat and sauté the onions and sweet potato for 3 minutes. Add the water, and cook for 5 minutes. Add the bell pepper, mushrooms, drained sun-dried tomatoes, and vinegar. Mix and cook for 1 minute.

2. Break the tempeh apart by hand into pea-size pieces and add them to the pan. Pour in the coconut aminos, maple syrup, seasoning, salt, and pepper. Reduce the heat to low and add a couple of tablespoons of water if the contents start sticking to the pan. Cook on low for 10 minutes.

3. Serve on gluten-free tortillas with your desired toppings: A drizzle of enchilada and cheese sauces, slices of avocado, halved cherry tomatoes, arugula, and any of your other favorite taco toppings.

INGREDIENT SMARTS: Sun-dried tomatoes come in two main varieties: Dried and packed in oil. The benefit of the oil-packed style is that they are ready to use and soft. The fully dried kind need to be rehydrated in warm water, unless you can find the ones in the plastic pouch that are soft.

Per Serving: Calories: 307; Fat: 19g; Saturated Fat: 3g; Cholesterol: 0mg; Carbohydrates: 28g; Fiber: 6g; Protein: 10g; Sodium: 148mg

Tamale Pie

NUT-FREE, SOY-FREE, CROWD-PLEASER

SERVES: 4 | **PREP TIME:** 20 minutes | **COOK TIME:** 40 minutes

How's this for a weeknight treat? Make it ahead and refrigerate for a quick mid-week heat-and-eat meal. A simply delicious cornbread topping is baked over cubed sweet potatoes, corn, beans, and a cumin and chili gravy. You can add any other veggies you like to make this tamale pie your own.

FOR THE FILLING

1 tablespoon extra-virgin olive oil

1 medium yellow onion, diced

1 garlic clove, minced

1 medium sweet potato, peeled and cubed

1 green bell pepper, seeded and diced

1 tablespoon chili powder

¼ teaspoon cayenne pepper (adjust for preference)

1 teaspoon ground cumin

1 (15-ounce) can black beans, drained and rinsed

1 (15-ounce) can diced tomatoes with juice

FOR THE CORNBREAD TOPPING

¾ cup cornmeal

¼ cup 1:1 all-purpose gluten-free flour, homemade (page 206) or store-bought

½ teaspoon baking powder

½ teaspoon table salt

¼ cup avocado oil

1 tablespoon pure maple syrup

¾ cup unsweetened gluten-free nondairy milk, homemade (page 218) or store-bought

1 teaspoon apple cider vinegar

1 (14-ounce) can corn, drained, divided

1. Preheat the oven to 400°F.

2. **To make the filling:** Heat the oil in a 9-inch cast iron skillet or large non-stick, oven-safe frying pan over medium heat. Add the onion and sauté for 5 minutes, until translucent. Add the garlic and sweet potato and cook, stirring occasionally, until the sweet potatoes can be easily pierced with a fork.

3. Add the green pepper, chili powder, cayenne pepper, and cumin. Cook for 1 minute, then add the black beans and diced tomatoes. Cook for 10 minutes. Remove from the heat.

4. To make the cornbread topping: In a large mixing bowl, while the filling simmers, whisk together the cornmeal, flour, baking powder, and salt. In a separate bowl or large measuring cup, whisk together the oil, maple syrup, milk, and vinegar.

5. Add the wet ingredients to the dry ingredients and mix until combined. Mix ½ cup of corn into the cornbread mixture, and spread the rest evenly on top of the filling in the skillet. Pour the cornmeal batter over the filling and bake for 20 to 25 minutes, until the top is golden brown. Remove from the oven, and let the pie sit in the pan for 10 minutes prior to serving.

Per Serving: Calories: 542; Fat: 20g; Saturated Fat: 3g; Cholesterol: 0mg; Carbohydrates: 81g; Fiber: 14g; Protein: 14g; Sodium: 577mg

Mojo Baked Jackfruit Nachos

NUT-FREE, SOY-FREE, CROWD-PLEASER

SERVES: 4 | **PREP TIME:** 15 minutes, not including
the Mojo Sauce | **COOK TIME:** 2 hours 30 minutes

This recipe uses young green jackfruit, which you can find in cans in the Asian aisle at the grocery store. The jackfruit is slow-roasted for a long time to turn meltingly tender, but that time is hands-off, and this recipe is great the next day, making it an ideal meal prep item. This recipe uses Mojo Sauce (page 222), a delectable Cuban-inspired combination of citrus and herbs.

1 (20-ounce) can young jackfruit in brine, drained

1 cup Mojo Sauce (page 222)

3 garlic cloves, minced

2 teaspoons liquid smoke

1 teaspoon pure maple syrup

2 teaspoons ground cumin

2 teaspoons smoked paprika

1 teaspoon chili powder (optional)

2 teaspoons kosher salt, plus more for topping

1 (15-ounce) can black beans, drained and rinsed

¼ cup chopped fresh cilantro

4 cups corn tortilla chips

Sliced avocado, for topping (optional)

Arugula, for topping (optional)

Freshly squeezed lime juice, for topping (optional)

1. Preheat the oven to 300°F.

2. In a large mixing bowl, combine the jackfruit, mojo sauce, garlic, liquid smoke, maple syrup, cumin, paprika, chili powder (if using), and salt. Transfer the mixture to an 8-by-8-inch baking dish, cover with aluminum foil, and bake for 2 to 4 hours.

3. Remove the dish from the oven. Use 2 forks to pull apart and separate the jackfruit into strands. Mix in the black beans and cilantro and bake for 30 minutes.

4. Serve with corn chips and other toppings, such as sliced avocado, arugula, and a spritz of lime juice and kosher salt to taste.

Per Serving: Calories: 369; Fat: 13g; Saturated Fat: 1g; Cholesterol: 0mg; Carbohydrates: 61g; Fiber: 5g; Protein: 5g; Sodium: 1,402mg

Corn Flour Zucchini Fritters

NUT-FREE, SOY-FREE, 30 MINUTES, CROWD-PLEASER,
WHOLE-FOOD PLANT-BASED

SERVES: 4 | **PREP TIME:** 20 minutes | **COOK TIME:** 10 minutes

The nutty flavor and aroma of toasted cornmeal combined with veggies makes a hard-to-resist meal in just 30 minutes. Masarepa flour is preferred for this recipe because it naturally binds together to form a more solid fritter, but you can use standard cornmeal and still enjoy delicious fritters.

1½ cups masarepa precooked white cornmeal

1 teaspoon onion powder

½ teaspoon garlic powder

½ cup canned corn, drained

1 cup shredded zucchini

1 (4-ounce) can diced green chiles

½ teaspoon table salt

1 cup water

½ cup coarse cornmeal

Avocado oil, for cooking (optional)

---

1. In a large mixing bowl, combine the masarepa, onion powder, garlic powder, corn, zucchini, green chiles, and salt. Pour in the water and mix until the dough comes together.

2. Divide the dough into 8 pieces, roll each piece into a ball, and then roll the balls in the cornmeal. Flatten each ball until it is roughly ½ inch thick.

3. Heat a griddle or large nonstick frying pan over high heat. Place the fritters on the hot surface; cook for 4 minutes on each side or until the fritters are golden brown. If your griddle is large enough, you can cook them all at once, or you can work in batches and store the cooked fritters in a 200°F oven to keep them warm. For extra-crispy fritters, add a little oil to the griddle or pan after the fritters have browned, and let them cook just until the edges are crispy.

4. Serve hot. These fritters are delicious served with a drizzle of Enchilada Sauce (page 214) or Lime Yogurt Sauce (page 60).

Per Serving: Calories: 236; Fat: 2g; Saturated Fat: 0g; Cholesterol: 0mg; Carbohydrates: 50g; Fiber: 5g; Protein: 6g; Sodium: 304mg

Quick Pad Thai

NUT-FREE, 30 MINUTES, CROWD-PLEASER

SERVES: 4 | **PREP TIME:** 10 minutes, plus 30 minutes
soaking time | **COOK TIME:** 10 minutes

Though pad thai sounds complicated, it's actually quick to make, and the veggies and garnishes used in it can be swapped based on what's available in your house. Think shredded carrots, crushed peanuts, and lime wedges—the list is endless. I always stock up on rice noodles because they cook fast, soak up sauce well, and have the perfect texture for a noodle bowl.

---

1 (14-ounce) package rice noodles

3 tablespoons avocado oil

1 (14-ounce) package firm tofu, cut into cubes

3 garlic cloves, minced

1 teaspoon sesame oil

¼ cup coconut aminos

3 tablespoons pure maple syrup

Juice of 1 lime (approximately 3 tablespoons)

1 teaspoon white vinegar

½ to 1 cup water

2 cups bean sprouts

½ cup shredded carrot

¼ cup chopped scallions (green parts only)

Crushed peanuts, for serving

Lime wedges, for serving

Chopped fresh chives, for serving (optional)

Chopped fresh cilantro, for serving (optional)

---

1. In a large bowl of warm water, soak the rice noodles without breaking them apart. Let them soak for at least 30 minutes but no longer than 1 hour.

2. Heat the oil in a large nonstick frying pan over medium-high heat. Tilt the pan slightly so the oil pools to one side, then add the tofu and return the pan to the burner. Shake the pan or move the tofu around with a spatula to coat the bottom of the pan with oil. Cook for 2 to 3 minutes, flip the tofu, and then continue to cook and flip until the tofu is golden brown on all sides.

3. Using a spatula, push the tofu to the side of the pan. Turn the heat to medium and add the garlic, sesame oil, coconut aminos, maple syrup, lime juice, and vinegar. Stir for 30 seconds, then add the soaked noodles. Toss to coat with the sauce, taking care not to break the tofu. Stir in ¼ cup of the water. Cook until the noodles are tender and the water has evaporated, about

3 minutes. If the noodles still aren't tender, stir in a little more water, ¼ cup at a time, and keep cooking until they reach your desired consistency.

4. Remove the pan from the heat, and toss the noodles and tofu with the bean sprouts, carrots, and scallions.

5. Serve each plate with a sprinkle of crushed peanuts, a lime wedge to spritz on, and a pinch of fresh chives and/or cilantro, if using.

INGREDIENT SMARTS: Tamarind paste is commonly used in pad thai, but it is a less common ingredient to have in your pantry. If you have tamarind, swap it in for the white vinegar, and add more as desired. Tamarind is sweet and tangy and can be found in most grocery stores in the international aisle.

Per Serving: Calories: 691; Fat: 21g; Saturated Fat: 3g; Cholesterol: 0mg; Carbohydrates: 101g; Fiber: 6g; Protein: 27g; Sodium: 500mg

CHAPTER 7

Weekend and Special Occasion Main Dishes

< Steamed Bao Buns with
Sticky Sesame–Oyster
Mushroom Filling,
page **164**

Gobi Manchurian

NUT-FREE, SOY-FREE, CROWD-PLEASER

SERVES: 4 | **PREP TIME:** 30 minutes | **COOK TIME:** 45 minutes

As the name suggests, Gobi Manchurian, a crispy baked cauliflower dish, is a fusion of Indian and Chinese flavors and cooking techniques. The result is a slightly crunchy, slightly spicy, sweet-and-sour creation that is great as a main dish with rice or as an appetizer, served with toothpicks. While the ingredients list for this recipe is lengthy, the process is very easy and worth it.

FOR THE SAUCE

2 tablespoons tomato paste

1 tablespoon apple cider vinegar

¼ cup diced red bell pepper

½ teaspoon cayenne pepper

1 tablespoon paprika

1 (4-ounce) can diced green chiles

1 tablespoon avocado oil

1 small yellow onion, chopped

2 tablespoons coconut aminos

1 tablespoon pure maple syrup

2 garlic cloves, chopped

2 tablespoons grated fresh ginger

¼ cup water

FOR THE CAULIFLOWER

1½ cups 1:1 all-purpose gluten-free flour, homemade (page 206) or store-bought

¼ cup cornstarch

½ teaspoon table salt

1 teaspoon baking powder

1 tablespoon tomato paste

2 cups unsweetened gluten-free nondairy milk, homemade (page 218) or store-bought

1 medium cauliflower head, cut into small florets

1. Preheat the oven to 450°F. Line a large rimmed baking sheet with parchment paper.

2. To make the sauce: In a blender or food processor, add the tomato paste, vinegar, bell pepper, cayenne pepper, paprika, green chiles, oil, onion, coconut aminos, maple syrup, garlic, ginger, and water and puree until smooth. Pour the sauce into a small pot and heat over medium until it begins to simmer. Cover the pot, reduce heat to low, and cook for 10 minutes, stirring occasionally, until the sauce is thickened. Remove from the heat and set aside.

3. To make the cauliflower: In a large mixing bowl, whisk together the flour, cornstarch, salt, baking powder, tomato paste, and milk. Using a fork, dip the cauliflower florets into the batter to coat. Place the coated florets on the prepared baking sheet. Bake for 15 minutes, flip each floret, then bake for an additional 10 minutes, until the cauliflower is browned and the batter is dry.

4. Pour the sauce over the florets, and flip them around until they are completely coated. Return the baking sheet to the oven and bake for 10 minutes, until the sauce is heated and bubbling. Serve immediately.

Per Serving: Calories: 404; Fat: 5g; Saturated Fat: 1g; Cholesterol: 0mg; Carbohydrates: 79g; Fiber: 6g; Protein: 12g; Sodium: 539mg

Cauliflower and Sweet Potato Crust Pizzas

NUT-FREE, SOY-FREE, CROWD-PLEASER

MAKES: 4 mini pizzas | **PREP TIME:** 20 minutes, not including cooking the sweet potato or cauliflower | **COOK TIME:** 20 minutes

Most cauliflower pizza crusts depend on cheese to keep them together, and it doesn't work well with vegan cheese. This recipe uses sweet potato, coarse cornmeal, and tapioca starch to make a crust that gets crisp and gives you that hidden serving of veggies. You can top your pizza with a multitude of options; this recipe gives you the base to build on.

2 tablespoons ground flaxseed

4 tablespoons water

½ small cauliflower head, cut into florets

1 large sweet potato

½ cup coarse cornmeal

¼ cup tapioca starch

1 teaspoon Italian seasoning

½ teaspoon onion powder

1 teaspoon kosher salt

1½ cups pizza sauce

2 cups vegan cheese

1. Preheat the oven to 400°F. Line 2 large rimmed baking sheets with parchment paper. Set aside.

2. In a small bowl, mix together the ground flaxseed and water. Set aside.

3. Bring a medium pot of water to a boil and add the cauliflower florets. Boil until just tender, about 5 minutes, then drain (or use a steamer basket and steam for about 10 minutes).

4. Prick the sweet potato all over with a fork, then microwave it for 5 minutes, until tender. (If you don't have a microwave, bake the potato at 425°F for 50 minutes.)

5. In a large bowl, mash together the baked sweet potato and steamed cauliflower using a heavy spoon or potato masher. Mix in the cornmeal, tapioca starch, Italian seasoning, onion powder, and salt. Stir to evenly combine. Fold in the soaked flaxseed. Knead the mixture in the bowl for a couple of minutes, until everything is evenly incorporated and the dough is smooth. Add more cornmeal if the dough feels too sticky.

6. Divide the dough into 4 equal pieces, and roll each piece into a ball. Using your hands, press each dough ball into a disk that is ½ inch thick and roughly 6 inches in diameter.

7. Heat a large nonstick frying pan over medium-high heat. Carefully add one rolled-out crust to the pan and cook for 5 minutes. Flip the crust and cook the other side for 5 minutes. If the dough sticks to the frying pan, continue to cook for another minute. Repeat with the remaining crusts.

8. Transfer the cooked crusts to the prepared baking sheets. Top each crust with sauce, cheese, and any other toppings. Bake for 15 minutes or until the cheese is melty.

MAKE AHEAD: This recipe calls for baked sweet potato and steamed cauliflower. These are two ingredients that can be made ahead and either refrigerated or frozen for future use. You can even prepare the sweet potato in the microwave or in an air fryer.

Per Serving (1 mini pizza): Calories: 403; Fat: 21g; Saturated Fat: 4g; Cholesterol: 0mg; Carbohydrates: 35g; Fiber: 6g; Protein: 19g; Sodium: 732mg

Sweet Potato and Black Bean Empanadas

NUT-FREE, SOY-FREE, CROWD-PLEASER

MAKES: 15 empanadas | **PREP TIME:** 1 hour, hash can be prepped ahead | **COOK TIME:** 20 minutes

Empanadas are a delicious, comforting, and surprisingly easy to prepare, once you've mastered making the gluten-free, vegan dough. You can get creative with fillings and use a variety of combinations like jalapeño, quinoa, and beans, or you can go sweet with a cinnamon and maple syrup–seasoned pumpkin filling.

2 tablespoons ground flaxseed

¼ cup room temperature water, plus ⅓ cup and 1 tablespoon ice water, plus more if needed, divided

2¼ cups 1:1 all-purpose gluten-free flour, homemade (page 206) or store-bought

1½ teaspoons table salt

8 tablespoons vegan butter, cold

1 tablespoon white vinegar

Sweet Potato Hash with Adobo (page 37), for the filling

1. In a small bowl, whisk together the flaxseed and ¼ cup of room-temperature water and set aside.

2. In a large mixing bowl, whisk together the flour and salt. Using a pastry cutter or 2 forks, cut the butter into the flour mixture until the butter is in pea-size chunks.

3. To the soaked flaxseed mixture, add the ⅓ cup plus 1 tablespoon of ice water and the vinegar. Pour the wet mixture into the bowl with the flour, and stir until the dough comes together, adding more ice water as needed until the dough holds together when you pinch it between your fingers. Cover the bowl with plastic wrap and refrigerate the dough while you prepare the fillings. (Or, if you're prepping ahead, refrigerate the dough overnight.)

4. Preheat the oven to 425°F. Line 2 large rimmed baking sheets with parchment paper. Set aside.

5. Prepare the Sweet Potato Hash with Adobo (page 37), or pull leftovers out of the refrigerator to use as the filling.

6. Divide the empanada dough into 15 equal pieces. Roll out each piece of dough into a 3-inch round, approximately ¼ inch thick, working with one piece of dough at a time and keeping the rest of the dough balls covered so they don't dry out.

7. Place approximately 2 tablespoons of filling in the middle of each dough round, positioning it a tad closer one side. Wet the edges of the dough with water, gently fold the dough over, and press together to seal. Press with the tines of a fork around the edge of the sealed dough, and transfer the empanadas to the prepared baking sheets, spacing them at least 1 inch apart.

8. Bake for 15 to 20 minutes or until the tops are golden brown.

Per Serving (1 empanada): Calories: 244; Fat: 8g; Saturated Fat: 1g; Cholesterol: 0mg; Carbohydrates: 36g; Fiber: 6g; Protein: 7g; Sodium: 452mg

Deconstructed Sushi Bowls

NUT-FREE, SOY-FREE

SERVES: 4 | **PREP TIME:** 30 minutes, plus 10 minutes
cooling time | **COOK TIME:** 18 minutes

Sushi is delicious and beautiful, but the required tools and skills can make it seem too daunting to attempt at home. These deconstructed bowls take away the work (and tools) but leave all the great flavors. The main element in these sushi bowls is the seasoned hearts of palm. The bowls are completely customizable, perfect for a family with various tastes. See the Change It Up tip for some customizing ideas.

FOR THE HEARTS OF PALM

1 (14-ounce) can hearts
  of palm, drained
  and chopped

2 tablespoons vegan mayo

2 teaspoons Old Bay
  seasoning

¼ teaspoon cayenne pepper

1 sheet nori, crushed

FOR THE SEASONED RICE

2 cups sushi rice

2¼ cups water

¼ cup seasoned rice vinegar

2 teaspoons sugar

1 teaspoon sea salt

1 sheet nori, crushed

FOR THE BOWL

¼ cup toasted
  sesame seeds

2 large avocados, cut
  into strips

1 medium carrot, julienne
  cut to 3-inch pieces

½ English cucumber,
  julienne cut to
  3-inch pieces

Sushi ginger, for serving
  (optional)

Wasabi, for serving
  (optional)

1. **To make the hearts of palm:** In a small bowl, mix together the hearts of palm, mayo, Old Bay, cayenne, and nori. Place the mixture in the refrigerator while you prepare the other ingredients.

2. **To make the seasoned rice:** In a large fine-mesh strainer, rinse the rice under cold water for 1 to 2 minutes, until the water runs clear. Shake the strainer to drain excess water. Place the rice in a large saucepan with the water,

bring to a simmer, reduce the heat to low, cover, and cook for 16 to 18 minutes. Remove from the heat, remove the cover, and let cool for 10 minutes.

3. Gently stir in the rice vinegar, sugar, and salt. Crush the nori into small flakes using your hands or a bowl and spoon. Sprinkle the flakes over the seasoned rice and fold the rice a couple of times to combine.

4. To make the bowls: Divide the rice among 4 bowls and top with toasted sesame seeds. Divide the avocado slices, carrot, and cucumber among the bowls and finish with the prepared hearts of palm. Serve with ginger and wasabi, if desired.

CHANGE IT UP: Your sushi bowls can be as creative as you want, and there are no limits on what you can add. Some great options include tempura sweet potatoes, daikon radish slices, vegan kimchi, or even breaded and fried jackfruit cakes.

Per Serving: Calories: 751; Fat: 23g; Saturated Fat: 4g; Cholesterol: 0mg; Carbohydrates: 123g; Fiber: 15g; Protein: 17g; Sodium: 665mg

Chili Mac and Cheese

NUT-FREE, SOY-FREE, CROWD-PLEASER

SERVES: 6 | **PREP TIME:** 40 minutes, not including Sunflower Seed
Cheese Sauce | **COOK TIME:** 30 minutes

Combine a quick, easy, high-protein chili recipe with homemade mac and cheese for an epic weekend comfort meal. This recipe works with a variety of gluten-free noodles, but I like shells the best for their retro appeal. The Sunflower Seed Cheese Sauce on page 210, works great, but in a pinch, you can swap in shredded vegan cheese or even an alfredo sauce.

½ cup water

½ cup dry texturized vegetable protein (TVP)

8 ounces gluten-free shell noodles

1½ cups Sunflower Seed Cheese Sauce (page 210), divided

½ onion, diced

2 garlic cloves, minced

1 tablespoon avocado oil

1 tablespoon gluten-free taco seasoning

2 teaspoons chili powder

½ jalapeño, diced, plus more for optional topping

1 (10-ounce) can diced tomatoes (like Rotel) (or 1¼ cups)

1 (15-ounce) can red kidney beans, drained and rinsed

Table salt

Freshly ground black pepper

Chopped scallions, for topping (optional)

Vegan sour cream, for topping (optional)

Shredded vegan cheddar, for topping (optional)

---

1. Preheat the oven to 425°F.

2. Bring the water to a boil in a large nonstick frying pan over high heat, then turn off the heat, stir in the TVP, cover the pan, and let it sit while you prepare the other ingredients. This amount of water won't look like much in the pan, but it is enough to rehydrate the TVP.

3. Bring a pot of water to a boil; cook the noodles for three-quarters of the time called for on the packaging, typically about 5 minutes. Drain the noodles in a colander, and rinse them under cool running water. Return the noodles to the pot and stir in 1 cup of the cheese sauce. Set aside.

4. Add the onion, garlic, oil, taco seasoning, chili powder, and jalapeño to the frying pan with the TVP, stir well, and heat over medium-high heat. Cook for 3 minutes, stirring. Mix in the tomatoes and beans, cover, and cook over medium heat for 7 minutes, until most of the liquid has been absorbed. Pour the noodles and cheese into the chili and fold a few times until everything is evenly incorporated. Add salt and pepper to taste.

5. If your frying pan is oven safe, top the mixture with the remaining ½ cup of cheese sauce and bake for 15 minutes, until it bubbles around the edges. If your pan is not oven safe, use a 9-by-13-inch glass baking dish. Top with scallions, vegan sour cream, additional jalapeño slices, and/or more cheese before serving.

Per Serving: Calories: 332; Fat: 9g; Saturated Fat: 0g; Cholesterol: 0mg; Carbohydrates: 54g; Fiber: 11g; Protein: 12g; Sodium: 449mg

BBQ Jackfruit Arepas

NUT-FREE, SOY-FREE, CROWD-PLEASER, WHOLE-FOOD PLANT-BASED

SERVES: 8 | **PREP TIME:** 30 minutes | **COOK TIME:** 30 minutes

Arepas are naturally gluten-free because the flour used, masarepa, is made only out of corn. Masarepa is made by grinding precooked, dehydrated corn kernels. You can find this type of cornmeal in the Mexican food aisle at most grocery stores. This Venezuelan and Columbian corn cake can be served like a pita pocket or as a thick tortilla. The natural sweetness of the arepas is a perfect complement to the crisped barbecue-flavored jackfruit.

---

2 (20-ounce) cans young jackfruit in water or brine (not syrup)

1 tablespoon smoked paprika

1 teaspoon chili powder

1 teaspoon ground cumin

½ teaspoon garlic powder

½ teaspoon onion powder

1 teaspoon kosher salt

1 teaspoon extra-virgin olive oil

1 cup vegan, gluten-free BBQ sauce, homemade (page 207) or store-bought

1 (15-ounce) can black beans, drained and rinsed

2½ cups water

2 cups masarepa pre-cooked white cornmeal

---

1. Preheat the oven to 425°F. Line a large rimmed baking sheet with parchment paper. Set aside.

2. Drain and rinse the jackfruit, then lay it out on a clean kitchen towel, fold the towel over the top, and press down to squeeze out as much water as possible. This process also separates the jackfruit strands.

3. In a large mixing bowl, whisk together the paprika, chili powder, ground cumin, garlic powder, onion powder, salt, and oil. Mix in the shredded jackfruit until it is evenly coated. Spread the jackfruit mixture on the prepared baking sheet and bake for 10 minutes. Remove from the oven, turn the jackfruit, and bake for another 10 minutes. Return the jackfruit to the bowl and mix with the BBQ sauce. Spread the coated jackfruit on the same parchment-lined baking sheet, return it to the oven, and bake for a final 10 minutes, until the jackfruit is slightly crisped on the edges. Turn off the oven, mix the black beans with the jackfruit, and place the baking sheet back in the turned-off oven until ready to serve.

4. While the jackfruit is baking, prepare the arepas. Pour the water into a large mixing bowl, then slowly sprinkle in the masarepa, stirring continuously. Knead the dough in the bowl or on the countertop until it is smooth and firm. Divide the dough into 8 equal pieces, roll each piece into a ball, and then use your hands to flatten the balls to a ½-inch thickness.

5. Cook the arepas on a hot griddle or nonstick pan over medium-high heat for 5 minutes on each side, then transfer them to a wire rack to cool. The outsides of the arepas should be firm to the touch and not sticky.

6. Use a dampened knife to open each arepa like a pita or split them in half. Fill the arepas with the jackfruit mixture before serving, or let people fill their own arepas at the table.

INGREDIENT SMARTS: Jackfruit is sold as two distinctly different canned varieties. The young green jackfruit in brine is used for savory dishes like this and has no distinct flavor. Jackfruit in syrup is the mature fruit; it resembles pineapple and is served as a dessert. If you find fresh jackfruit in the store, it is more than likely the mature, sweet version and is not a suitable ingredient for this recipe.

Per Serving: Calories: 315; Fat: 4g; Saturated Fat: 1g; Cholesterol: 0mg; Carbohydrates: 60g; Fiber: 9g; Protein: 16g; Sodium: 650mg

Veggie Pot Pie

NUT-FREE, SOY-FREE, CROWD-PLEASER

SERVES: 8 | **PREP TIME:** 45 minutes, plus 15 minutes
cooling time | **COOK TIME:** 45 minutes

Pot pie is classic comfort food, and this from-scratch recipe is both satisfying and easier to make than you'd imagine. I opted for a double-crust pie, so you get lots of the flaky, delicious crust along with the creamy vegetable and tofu filling. You can make this in a pie dish, or you can shape it into individual, handheld pot pies. This is also a great make-ahead dish for a dinner party.

FOR THE CRUST

2 cups 1:1 all-purpose gluten-free flour, homemade (page 206) or store-bought

1 teaspoon table salt

⅔ cup shortening or chilled vegan butter, frozen

6 to 8 tablespoons ice water, divided

FOR THE FILLING

⅓ cup vegan butter

1 small yellow onion, diced

1 celery stalk, diced

1 cup frozen mixed veggies

⅓ cup 1:1 all-purpose gluten-free flour, homemade (page 206) or store-bought

1 cup unsweetened gluten-free nondairy milk, homemade (page 218) or store-bought, plus extra for brushing

¾ cup low-sodium vegetable stock

1 tablespoon nutritional yeast

2 tablespoons vegan cream cheese

½ teaspoon table salt

½ teaspoon garlic powder

¼ teaspoon dried thyme

1 teaspoon ground sage

1 (14-ounce) package firm or extra-firm tofu, cut into ¼-inch cubes

1. Preheat the oven to 400°F.

2. To make the crust: In a large bowl, whisk together the flour and salt. Cut in thin pieces of the shortening using a pastry cutter or 2 forks. Stir using a heavy wooden spoon to coat the shortening with the flour, until the mix resembles fine gravel.

3. Sprinkle 1 tablespoon of ice water at a time into the bowl and then use a heavy spoon to mix the dough; stir gently until there are no dry spots remaining. Take care not to overwork the dough, which will make it tough.

4. Turn the dough onto the counter, divide it in half, and press each piece into thick, round disks. Wrap separately in plastic wrap and refrigerate for at least 15 minutes while you make the filling.

5. To make the filling: In a large, nonstick frying pan or pot, melt the butter over medium-low heat. Sauté the onion and celery for 2 to 3 minutes or until the onion is translucent but not browned. Stir in the mixed veggies. Sprinkle the flour over the mixture, and stir to coat evenly. Add the milk, stock, nutritional yeast, cheese, salt, garlic powder, thyme, and sage, and stir while heating for 5 minutes or until the mixture is thick and bubbling. Remove from the heat and gently stir in the cubed tofu.

6. Remove the dough from the refrigerator. Place a sheet of parchment paper on the counter, set one piece of dough in the center, and place another sheet of parchment paper on top. Roll into a round that is ¼ inch thick and about 10 inches in diameter. Remove the top parchment sheet, flip the rolled dough into a 9-inch pie dish, remove the parchment, and fill with the veggie filling.

7. Roll out the second sheet of dough between layers of parchment. Place the top dough on and press the edges to seal. Brush the top with a little nondairy milk, cut a few vent slits in the top. Bake for 35 to 40 minutes, until the top is browned. Let rest for 15 minutes before serving.

CHANGE IT UP: To make individual hand pies, divide the dough into 8 equal pieces, roll the pieces out into thin rounds, fill them like calzones, and bake them for 20 minutes.

Per Serving: Calories: 447; Fat: 26g; Saturated Fat: 5g; Cholesterol: 0mg; Carbohydrates: 44g; Fiber: 3g; Protein: 10g; Sodium: 507mg

Sweet Potato and Corn Falafel

NUT-FREE, SOY-FREE, CROWD-PLEASER

MAKES: 30 falafel balls | **PREP TIME:** 20 minutes, plus overnight soaking | **COOK TIME:** 35 minutes

This falafel recipe is a sweet and earthy twist on the traditional Middle Eastern dish. Baked or fried, they can be served on their own as a snack, paired with homemade Hummus (page 208) for a dish-emptying appetizer, or added to a wrap or grain bowl for a complete meal.

1½ cups dried chickpeas

1 medium sweet potato

1 small red onion, diced

3 garlic cloves, chopped

1 cup fresh cilantro leaves

2 tablespoons freshly squeezed lemon juice

2 teaspoons ground cumin

½ tablespoon smoked paprika

1 teaspoon table salt

1 teaspoon baking powder

1 (14-ounce) can corn kernels, drained and rinsed

3 tablespoons avocado oil, divided

1. In a large bowl, cover the dried chickpeas with about 2 inches of water; allow the chickpeas to soak overnight on the counter. Drain and rinse them before using.

2. Preheat the oven to 375°F.

3. Pierce the sweet potato all over with a fork, then microwave on high for 8 minutes or until it is soft all the way through. Slice the cooked sweet potato in half, scoop the flesh into a large mixing bowl, and discard the skin. Using a potato masher, mash the sweet potato flesh; set aside.

4. In a high-speed blender or food processor, combine the rinsed chickpeas, onion, garlic, cilantro, lemon juice, cumin, smoked paprika, salt, and baking powder. Process until the mixture forms a rough meal. You should still be able to see some large pieces of chickpea throughout. Fold the mixture, along with the corn, into the sweet potato.

5. Line a large rimmed baking sheet with parchment paper, and brush half of the oil onto the paper. Use 2 spoons or an ice cream scoop to evenly divide and form the falafel mixture into about 30 (1-inch) balls. Place the balls on the prepared baking sheet and gently flatten the tops with the back of a spoon. Brush the remaining oil on top of the flattened falafel balls.

6. Bake for 15 minutes, flip the falafels, and then bake for another 10 minutes, until the falafels are lightly golden and firm to the touch.

CHANGE IT UP: To pan-fry the falafel, heat the oil in a large skillet over medium-high heat. Cook the flattened falafel balls in batches of 5, making sure not to crowd the pan. Cook for 3 to 4 minutes on each side, then transfer to a plate lined with paper towels. The falafels should be golden and crunchy on the outside, warm and dense on the inside. Add more oil as needed for each batch.

Per Serving (3 balls): Calories: 198; Fat: 7g; Saturated Fat: 5g; Cholesterol: 0mg; Carbohydrates: 29g; Fiber: 1g; Protein: 8g; Sodium: 323mg

Pizza Boats with Eggplant and Chickpeas

NUT-FREE, SOY-FREE, CROWD-PLEASER

SERVES: 4 | **PREP TIME:** 45 minutes, plus 45 minutes
dough rising time | **COOK TIME:** 45 minutes

Turkish pide or "pizza boats" can be filled with anything you can imagine, making them the perfect meal for a family with different taste preferences. The soft yeast dough is easy to prepare, and you'll be eating your pizza boats in less than 2 hours.

3½ cups 1:1 all-purpose gluten-free flour, homemade (page 206) or store-bought

1 tablespoon instant dry yeast

1 tablespoon sugar

1½ teaspoons kosher salt

¾ cup warm water

¼ cup unsweetened gluten-free nondairy milk, homemade (page 218) or store-bought

2 tablespoons vegan butter, melted, plus more for brushing

1 yellow onion, finely chopped

1 tablespoon extra-virgin olive oil

2 garlic cloves, finely chopped

1 teaspoon ground cumin

½ teaspoon smoked paprika

½ teaspoon ground cinnamon

½ teaspoon red pepper flakes

1 medium eggplant, cut into ½-inch cubes

1 (15-ounce) can petite diced tomatoes

1 (15-ounce) can chickpeas, drained

---

1. In a large bowl, mix together the flour, yeast, sugar, and salt. Pour in the water, milk, and melted butter. Use a heavy wooden spoon to mix the dough until it comes together. Turn the dough onto a lightly floured countertop and knead for 5 minutes. Place the dough in a lightly oiled bowl, cover, and let rise for 30 to 45 minutes.

2. While the dough is rising, prepare the eggplant filling. In a large nonstick frying pan, combine the onion and oil, and sauté for 10 minutes over medium heat. Add the garlic, cumin, paprika, cinnamon, and red pepper, and sauté for 3 minutes.

3. Add the chopped eggplant, stir, and sauté for 2 minutes. Add the chopped tomatoes and chickpeas, mix, cover, and cook over low heat for 15 minutes. Let cool while the dough finishes rising. Preheat the oven to 425°F.

4. Turn the dough out onto a lightly floured surface and divide into 4 equal pieces. Shape each piece into a ball. Use a rolling pin to flatten each ball into an oval about 10 inches long by 8 inches wide and ¼ inch to ⅛ inch thick. Roll the long sides in about an inch to form the "boat" edges, then fold in about ½ inch of the dough on each short end and pinch the ends tightly together. It should resemble a boat with a center open for filling.

5. Transfer the shaped dough boats to a parchment-lined pan, and fill each with the eggplant filling.

6. Bake for 15 to 20 minutes or until the edges are light golden brown. Rotate the pan halfway through for even baking. Remove the pizzas from the oven, brush the edges with butter or oil, and allow them to cool for 5 minutes before serving.

Per Serving: Calories: 759; Fat: 13g; Saturated Fat: 2g; Cholesterol: 0mg; Carbohydrates: 144g; Fiber: 14g; Protein: 17g; Sodium: 832mg

Steamed Bao Buns with Sticky Sesame–Oyster Mushroom Filling

NUT-FREE, SOY-FREE

MAKES: 10 buns | **PREP TIME:** 30 minutes, plus 1 hour dough rising | **COOK TIME:** 15 minutes

Bao buns, otherwise known as steamed buns (but literally translated as "bun buns"), make a great Chinese-inspired alternative to taco night. Traditionally filled with pork, these buns let you get creative with sauces, fillings, and veggies. I love them with pan-seared oyster mushrooms in a sweet-and-sour glaze. The buns and the sauce pair wonderfully with a side of pickled veggies and crunchy broccoli slaw.

2 teaspoons instant dry yeast

3 cups 1:1 all-purpose gluten-free flour, homemade (page 206) or store-bought

2 teaspoons xanthan gum

1 tablespoon sugar

1 teaspoon table salt

1 teaspoon baking powder

1 cup warm water

3 tablespoons avocado oil, divided

½ cup coconut aminos

2 tablespoons rice vinegar

2 tablespoons pure maple syrup

2 teaspoons sesame oil

2 teaspoons gluten-free sriracha sauce (optional)

1 teaspoon liquid smoke

1 pound (4 cups) oyster mushrooms, cut into ½-inch-thick pieces

2 cups bagged broccoli and carrot slaw

1. In a large bowl, whisk together the yeast, flour, xanthan gum, sugar, salt, and baking powder. Pour in the water and 1 tablespoon of oil. Mix using a heavy spoon until the dough comes together. Turn the dough out onto a lightly floured surface and knead for 8 minutes. The dough should be smooth. Place the dough in a lightly oiled bowl, cover, and let rise for 1 hour.

2. Divide the dough in half, keeping one half in the covered bowl, and cut the other half into 5 pieces. Roll each piece into a ball, then use your hands to flatten the balls to a 1-inch thickness. Use a rolling pin to roll the disks into 5-inch rounds. Brush the tops with an additional tablespoon of oil, fold the dough disks in half, and place each shaped bun on a little piece of parchment paper; let the buns rest on a baking sheet for about 15 minutes. Repeat the process with the remaining dough until all 10 bao buns are shaped, placed on pieces of parchment paper, and allowed to rest for 15 minutes.

3. Transfer the bao buns to a steamer (bamboo or other), leaving the parchment paper attached and working in batches to avoid crowding or touching. Steam the buns for 8 minutes.

4. While the buns steam, cook the mushrooms. In a small bowl, whisk together the coconut aminos, rice vinegar, maple syrup, sesame oil, sriracha, and liquid smoke. Set aside.

5. In a large nonstick frying pan, heat the remaining oil over medium-high heat, add the mushrooms in an even layer, and cook for 3 minutes without stirring. Flip the mushrooms and cook for an additional 3 minutes or until they are lightly browned.

6. Pour in the sauce and flip the mushrooms to coat. Cook for 3 minutes or until the sauce is thick. Turn off the heat, fill each bao bun with the mushrooms, and top with the slaw.

TECHNIQUE TIP: When steaming dough, make sure to use parchment paper under the dough because it will stick. If you don't have a steamer, you can create one! Crumple up three pieces of aluminum foil into golf ball–size rounds, and place them on the bottom of a deep frying pan or pot. Place a heat-safe plate or small wire rack on top of the foil balls, and pour in enough water to come halfway up the aluminum balls. Put the pan over medium-high heat, bring the water to a simmer, and cover the pan or pot to steam. Add more water as needed between batches.

Per Serving (1 bun): Calories: 265; Fat: 7g; Saturated Fat: 1g; Cholesterol: 0mg; Carbohydrates: 47g; Fiber: 3g; Protein: 6g; Sodium: 478mg

Bang Bang "Shrimp"

NUT-FREE, SOY-FREE, CROWD-PLEASER

SERVES: 4 | **PREP TIME:** 20 minutes | **COOK TIME:** 25 minutes

In this recipe, hearts of palm take the place of shrimp to recreate this super-popular Asian-inspired dish. These little fiery nuggets can be served with rice or gluten-free noodles, or even as a salad topping or taco filling.

½ cup vegan mayo

¼ cup sweet chili sauce

2 tablespoons gluten-free sriracha sauce

½ tablespoon rice wine vinegar

1 teaspoon sesame oil

3 tablespoons avocado oil, divided

½ cup unsweetened gluten-free nondairy milk, homemade (page 218) or store-bought

1 tablespoon apple cider vinegar

1 (14-ounce) can hearts of palm

½ cup gluten-free panko breadcrumbs

6 tablespoons potato starch, divided

1 teaspoon Old Bay Seasoning

½ teaspoon garlic powder

½ teaspoon table salt

¼ teaspoon baking soda

½ cup rice flour

Sesame seeds, for topping (optional)

Scallion, diced for topping (optional)

Red pepper flakes, for topping (optional)

1. In a small bowl, whisk together the vegan mayo, sweet chili sauce, sriracha, rice wine vinegar, and sesame oil. Set aside while you prepare the "shrimp."

2. Preheat the oven to 375°F. Line a large rimmed baking sheet with parchment paper, and brush the parchment with 1½ tablespoons of avocado oil. Set aside.

3. In a small mixing bowl, combine the milk and apple cider vinegar and set it aside. Don't be alarmed to see it thicken and curdle; you've just made vegan buttermilk!

4. Drain and rinse the hearts of palm before cutting them into ½-inch pieces and setting aside.

5. Stir the panko breadcrumbs, 3 tablespoons of potato starch, Old Bay seasoning, garlic powder, salt, and baking soda into the milk and vinegar mixture. Put the rice flour and remaining 3 tablespoons of potato starch in their own small bowl.

6. Dredge each piece of the hearts of palm in the rice flour, then the panko and milk mixture. Then, dredge each piece through the rice flour again, followed by the panko and milk mixture. Place the coated pieces on the prepared baking sheet.

7. Bake for 15 minutes, then brush the tops of the coated shrimp with the remaining 1½ tablespoons of avocado oil. Flip the shrimp and bake for 10 more minutes, until golden and crunchy.

8. Remove the shrimp from the oven, toss them in the bang bang sauce, and serve immediately.

Per Serving: Calories: 483; Fat: 9g; Saturated Fat: 3g; Cholesterol: 0mg; Carbohydrates: 62g; Fiber: 5g; Protein: 22g; Sodium: 584mg

Zucchini Lasagna Pockets

NUT-FREE, CROWD-PLEASER, WHOLE-FOOD PLANT-BASED

SERVES: 4 | **PREP TIME:** 45 minutes, plus 15 minutes cooling time | **COOK TIME:** 1 hour

Vegan, gluten-free lasagna can be a tricky dish to execute; most recipes swap in slices of zucchini for noodles, which makes for a watery casserole. In my version, I solve the watery zucchini problem by making individual lasagna pockets. Once you master the technique, you'll be sure to keep this recipe in your regular mealtime rotation.

2 cups marinara
sauce, divided

1 (14-ounce) package
firm tofu

2 teaspoons
nutritional yeast

1 tablespoon yellow
miso paste

1 teaspoon table salt

½ teaspoon onion powder

1 teaspoon tapioca starch

1 large zucchini
(approximately 14 inches
in length and 4 inches in
diameter)

1. Preheat the oven to 425°F. Spread ½ cup of marinara in the bottom of a 9-by-13-inch glass baking sheet. Set aside.

2. Drain the water from the tofu tub and squeeze the tofu using your hands to remove as much water as possible. It's okay if your tofu block cracks or breaks because you will be crushing it later in the recipe.

3. In a medium bowl, combine the drained tofu, nutritional yeast, miso paste, salt, onion powder, and tapioca starch. Mash using a potato masher, pastry cutter, or heavy spoon. You want your tofu to be in small pieces and have the same look and texture as ricotta. Using a food processor will break it down too much. Set the filling aside, or cover it and refrigerate for later.

4. Peel the outer layer of the zucchini. Using a vegetable peeler, make long strips of zucchini that are the full width of your vegetable peeler. Stop when you reach the watery center of the zucchini.

5. Lay 2 strips of zucchini on your work space, and weave in 2 additional strips so that it looks like a four-box checkerboard. Place ¼ cup of the tofu filling in the center of the zucchini weave, then alternate folding the strips to make a rough woven look on top. Flip the filled zucchini square and carefully place it in the prepared baking dish. Repeat until the baking dish is filled with 4 filled zucchini squares.

6. Pour the remaining 1½ cups of marinara over the zucchini squares, cover the baking dish with aluminum foil, and bake for 45 minutes. Remove the foil and bake for an additional 15 minutes. Remove the zucchini pockets from the oven, and let them cool in the pan for 15 to 20 minutes before serving.

TECHNIQUE TIP: The purpose of weaving together the zucchini strips is to make serving easier. You can skip the weaving and make a standard lasagna, replacing regular noodles with the zucchini strips. However, the individual squares are more fun, and you don't have to worry about messy cutting and serving.

Per Serving: Calories: 199; Fat: 10g; Saturated Fat: 1g; Cholesterol: 0mg; Carbohydrates: 15g; Fiber: 5g; Protein: 19g; Sodium: 818mg

Tofu Tikka Masala

NUT-FREE, CROWD-PLEASER

SERVES: 4 | **PREP TIME:** 15 minutes, plus 5 minutes
resting time | **COOK TIME:** 45 minutes

This recipe is made by slow-cooking curry spices in a base of tomato and coconut cream with browned onions, garlic, tofu, and a lot of ginger. The end result is a warming, aromatic, and deeply rich dish that can be served in a variety of ways and paired with many vegetables, such as snow peas, broccoli, and/or cauliflower.

2 cups water

1 cup uncooked jasmine or basmati rice

1 (14-ounce) package extra-firm tofu

4 cups low-sodium vegetable stock, divided

1 tablespoon nutritional yeast

1 tablespoon avocado oil

1 medium yellow onion, diced

3 garlic cloves, minced

1 tablespoon paprika

1 tablespoon ground turmeric

1 tablespoon ground coriander

2 teaspoons ground cumin

1 tablespoon soy sauce

1 (13.5-ounce) can full-fat coconut milk

1 (15-ounce) can petite diced tomatoes

2 tablespoons grated fresh ginger

¼ cup minced fresh cilantro, divided

Scallion, chopped (green parts only), for serving

1. In a small pot, bring the water to a boil and stir in the rice. Reduce the heat to low, cover, and cook for 15 to 20 minutes or until the rice is tender. Remove from the heat and keep covered. The rice can be cooked ahead of time or while you're making the sauce.

2. Cut the block of tofu into ½- to ¼-inch cubes. Transfer the tofu cubes to a medium pot, spreading them out in a single layer, and heat them over medium-high heat. Cook for 5 minutes, then gently flip the tofu and cook for an additional 5 minutes. Pour 2 cups of the vegetable stock and the nutritional yeast into the pot and cook for 5 minutes. Use a spatula to gently release the tofu from the bottom of the pot.

3. Pour the oil into the pot, stir gently, and then add the onion and garlic. Reduce the heat to medium-low and cook for 10 minutes, stirring occasionally with to avoid scorching. The onions should be translucent and just beginning to brown. While this is cooking, prepare the remaining ingredients.

4. In a small bowl, whisk together the paprika, turmeric, coriander, and cumin. Set aside. In a separate bowl, whisk together the soy sauce, coconut milk, tomatoes, and the remaining 2 cups of stock. Set aside.

5. Add the grated ginger to the pot, stir, and cook for 30 seconds. Sprinkle the spices into the pot, flip the tofu, and stir to coat the tofu and onions; cook for 30 seconds. Pour in the soy sauce mixture. Stir for 1 minute or until the sauce is heated through. Cook over medium-low heat for 15 minutes. Mix in half of the cilantro, remove the pot from the heat, and let it sit for 5 minutes before serving.

6. Serve the tofu and sauce over cooked rice, topped with the remaining cilantro and chopped scallions.

CHANGE IT UP: To spice up this dish, add 1 teaspoon of cayenne pepper with the other spices. Cayenne adds heat and complements the earthy flavors of the turmeric and cumin.

Per Serving: Calories: 521; Fat: 30g; Saturated Fat: 19g; Cholesterol: 0mg; Carbohydrates: 53g; Fiber: 6g; Protein: 16g; Sodium: 286mg

Baked Popcorn Cauliflower

NUT-FREE, SOY-FREE, CROWD-PLEASER

SERVES: 4 | **PREP TIME:** 30 minutes | **COOK TIME:** 25 to 30 minutes

When people refer to popcorn cauliflower, they typically mean bite-size fried cauliflower florets. In order to make this recipe a bit more interesting—and healthy—I took a more literal approach and used popped popcorn as the crispy coating. The silken tofu adds a complete protein, as well as an excellent base for the coating.

1 cup 1:1 all-purpose gluten-free flour, homemade (page 206) or store-bought, divided

1 (12-ounce) container soft silken tofu

¾ cup water

1 tablespoon nutritional yeast

1 teaspoon table salt

½ teaspoon onion powder

½ teaspoon garlic powder

6 cups popped popcorn (see Ingredient Smarts tip)

1 medium cauliflower head, cut into 1-inch florets

1 teaspoon Italian seasoning

Nonstick cooking spray

1. Preheat the oven to 450°F. Line a rimmed baking sheet with parchment.

2. In a medium bowl, whisk together ½ cup of the flour, tofu, water, nutritional yeast, salt, onion powder, and garlic powder. Set aside.

3. In a food processor, combine the popped popcorn, remaining ½ cup flour, and Italian seasoning. Process until the popcorn is broken into sand-like pieces. Transfer them to a medium bowl.

4. Coat the cauliflower in the tofu mixture, then toss with the popcorn mixture.

5. Place the florets on the prepared baking sheet and bake for 15 minutes. Mist them with cooking spray, flip, and bake for 10 to 15 minutes longer. Serve immediately.

INGREDIENT SMARTS: You can use either air-popped popcorn or popcorn cooked in oil for this recipe. Avoid using microwave popcorn, though, because it's not as good for you or for this recipe.

Per Serving: Calories: 282; Fat: 5g; Saturated Fat: 1g; Cholesterol: 0mg; Carbohydrates: 50g; Fiber: 6g; Protein: 12g; Sodium: 634mg

Soy Curl–Stuffed Squash

SERVES: 4 | **PREP TIME:** 20 minutes | **COOK TIME:** 1 hour

This recipe combines the savory flavors of sage, garlic, and onion with the natural sweetness of acorn squash. The squash halves make beautiful individual servings.

- 2 acorn squash, halved lengthwise and center scooped clean
- 1 tablespoon extra-virgin olive oil
- ¼ teaspoon table salt
- 1 cup dried soy curls
- 2 cups warm water
- 2 teaspoons poultry seasoning
- ½ teaspoon paprika
- 1 tablespoon coconut aminos
- 2 cups chopped kale
- 8 ounces button mushrooms, sliced
- 1 shallot, diced
- 2 garlic cloves, minced
- 1 pint cherry tomatoes, halved
- Balsamic reduction, for serving

---

1. Preheat the oven to 400°F. Line a rimmed baking sheet with parchment.

2. Place the squash halves on the baking sheet, cut-side up. Drizzle with the oil, then sprinkle with the salt. Rub the oil into the squash, then turn the squash cut-sides down. Bake for 35 to 40 minutes, until the flesh is tender. Remove the squash from the oven, and leave the oven on.

3. While the squash cooks, combine the soy curls and water in a small mixing bowl. Let the curls sit for 5 minutes, then drain the water from the bowl. Chop the soy curls into small pieces, and return them to the bowl. Mix the chopped soy curls with the poultry seasoning, paprika, and coconut aminos. Set aside.

4. In a large nonstick frying pan over medium-high heat, cook the kale, mushrooms, shallot, and garlic until the kale has wilted, about 5 minutes. Add the cherry tomatoes and soy curls, toss to combine, and cook for 3 minutes.

5. Turn the acorn squash cut-sides up, fill with the cooked filling, and bake for 15 minutes. Drizzle with balsamic reduction before serving.

Per Serving: Calories: 248; Fat: 5g; Saturated Fat: 1g; Cholesterol: 0mg; Carbohydrates: 40g; Fiber: 5g; Protein: 18g; Sodium: 225mg

CHAPTER 8

Baked Goods, Desserts, and Treats

Flourless Chocolate Cake

NUT-FREE, SOY-FREE, CROWD-PLEASER

SERVES: 12 | **PREP TIME:** 30 minutes | **BAKE TIME:** 1 hour, plus overnight chilling

Many novice home cooks shy away from making cake because it just sounds complicated. I hope you'll find that this cake is just the opposite: It's decadent and foolproof. You'll be bringing this out at parties in no time.

Nonstick cooking spray

3 tablespoons ground flaxseed

½ cup water

2 cups vegan bittersweet or dark chocolate (66% or more cacao), divided (1 cup for the cake and 1 cup for optional ganache)

1 cup no-added-sugar applesauce

½ cup vegan sugar

½ cup unsweetened cocoa powder

1 tablespoon instant coffee or instant espresso granules

1 teaspoon pure vanilla extract

½ teaspoon sea salt

¼ cup unsweetened gluten-free nondairy milk, homemade (page 218) or store-bought (optional)

Vegan powdered sugar, for serving

Fresh berries, for serving

1. Place a rack in middle of the oven and preheat it to 350°F.

2. Place an 8- or 9-inch springform or cake pan on a piece of parchment paper, trace the bottom, and cut just inside the line to form a liner for your pan. Spray the pan lightly with cooking spray, then place the parchment circle in the bottom and spray the top of the paper with cooking spray; set the prepared pan aside.

3. In a small bowl, mix together the ground flaxseed and water. Set aside to soak.

4. Chop the chocolate into small pieces. Using a double boiler or a microwave, melt the chocolate until smooth. If using the microwave, heat and stir in 30-second intervals. If using a double boiler, bring the water to a gentle simmer and place the chocolate in the top level (or in a Pyrex or metal bowl over a small pot—but don't let the bowl touch the water), stirring frequently.

5. In a large bowl, mix together the applesauce, sugar, cocoa powder, instant coffee, vanilla, and salt. Fold in the soaked flaxseed, then the melted chocolate.

6. Pour the batter into the prepared pan. Shake the pan gently to even out the thick batter.

7. Bake on the middle rack of the oven for 55 to 60 minutes. To check if the cake is done, jiggle the pan. If the middle is set, then the cake is finished baking. A larger pan will take less time, while a smaller pan might take longer.

8. Allow the cake to cool to room temperature, cover with foil or plastic wrap, and refrigerate for a few hours or ideally overnight.

9. After the cake has chilled, remove the outer ring of the springform pan; either leave the cake on the base of the pan or use the parchment paper to carefully transfer the cake to a serving dish.

10. To make the optional ganache, in a medium microwave-safe bowl, mix together the remaining cup of vegan chocolate chips with the milk. Microwave the mixture for 30 seconds, stir, and then microwave for 30 seconds more. Repeat until the chocolate is melted.

11. To serve, dust a little powdered sugar on top of the cake, top with fresh berries, and/or drizzle with ganache.

Per Serving: Calories: 219; Fat: 13g; Saturated Fat: 7g; Cholesterol: 1mg; Carbohydrates: 26g; Fiber: 5g; Protein: 3g; Sodium: 85mg

Chocolate Mug Cake

NUT-FREE, SOY-FREE, 30 MINUTES, CROWD-PLEASER

SERVES: 1 | **PREP TIME:** 5 minutes | **BAKE TIME:** 1 minute

A mug cake is a great recipe for when you want dessert but don't need a whole cake. This recipe will satisfy your sweet tooth in under 5 minutes, requiring only a measuring cup, a mug, and a spoon. The result is a gooey, chocolatey, and rich treat. This recipe includes an optional chocolate glaze, but another delicious and even simpler topping is a tablespoon of peanut butter.

FOR THE CAKE

3 tablespoons gluten-free oat flour (see Ingredient Smarts tip)

1½ tablespoons unsweetened cocoa powder

1 teaspoon safflower or avocado oil

1 tablespoon pure maple syrup

¼ teaspoon baking powder

¼ teaspoon pure vanilla extract

Pinch table salt

2 tablespoons unsweetened gluten-free nondairy milk, homemade (page 218) or store-bought

FOR THE OPTIONAL GLAZE

2 teaspoons unsweetened cocoa powder

3 teaspoons unsweetened gluten-free nondairy milk, homemade (page 218) or store-bought

1 teaspoon pure maple syrup

1. To make the cake: In a small bowl, whisk together the flour, cocoa powder, oil, maple syrup, baking powder, vanilla, salt, and milk. Pour the batter into a large mug (the cake will nearly triple in size as it cooks) and microwave for 1 minute, until the cake has puffed up.

2. To make the glaze: Whisk together the cocoa powder, milk, and maple syrup. Pour over the top of the warm cake, if desired, and enjoy.

INGREDIENT SMARTS: You can make your own oat flour by pulsing oats in a food processor or blender. This is a great tip if you need gluten-free oat flour but are unable to find any.

TECHNIQUE TIP: If you prefer, mix the batter in an oven-safe ramekin and cook your mug cake in an air fryer at 350°F for 3 minutes.

Per Serving: Calories: 193; Fat: 7g; Saturated Fat: 1g; Cholesterol: 0mg; Carbohydrates: 32g; Fiber: 4g; Protein: 4g; Sodium: 164mg

Rice Pudding

NUT-FREE, SOY-FREE, 30 MINUTES, CROWD-PLEASER,
WHOLE-FOOD PLANT-BASED

SERVES: 4 | **PREP TIME:** 5 minutes | **COOK TIME:** 5 minutes

Rice pudding is a comforting, nostalgic treat. And the added bonuses are that the ingredients are minimal and you can make it in under 10 minutes. Use any rice to make this recipe, but I prefer jasmine or basmati because the individual grains keep their chew.

---

1 cup unsweetened gluten-free nondairy milk, homemade (page 218) or store-bought

¼ cup raisins

2 tablespoons pure maple syrup

1 tablespoon chia seeds

1 teaspoon ground cinnamon

Pinch table salt

2 cups cooked jasmine rice

In a small pot over medium-high heat, mix together the milk, raisins, maple syrup, chia seeds, cinnamon, and salt. Bring the mixture to a simmer, about 5 minutes, then remove the pot from the heat and stir in the cooked rice. Cover and let rest for 2 minutes. Serve warm or chilled.

Per Serving: Calories: 227; Fat: 3g; Saturated Fat: 1g; Cholesterol: 5mg; Carbohydrates: 47g; Fiber: 2g; Protein: 5g; Sodium: 70mg

Mix-in-the-Dish Pumpkin Pie

SOY-FREE, CROWD-PLEASER

SERVES: 8 | **PREP TIME:** 20 minutes, plus at least 2 hours
cooling time | **BAKE TIME:** 1 hour 5 minutes

This recipe will appeal to all the clean-up crews out there. The almond flour–based pie crust mixes up directly in the dish! No mixing bowls and no counter splatter involved. The pumpkin pie filling, though not as tidy to prepare, is custardy, simple, and delicious.

FOR THE CRUST

1 cup 1:1 all-purpose gluten-free flour, homemade (page 206) or store-bought

½ cup almond flour

1 tablespoon vegan sugar

1 teaspoon table salt

⅓ cup melted vegan butter

1 to 3 tablespoons unsweetened gluten-free nondairy milk, homemade (page 218) or store-bought

FOR THE FILLING

2½ cups pumpkin puree (you'll use about 1½ cans)

¼ cup vegan brown sugar

¼ cup pure maple syrup

¾ cup unsweetened gluten-free nondairy milk, homemade (page 218) or store-bought

1 teaspoon pure vanilla extract

2 teaspoons pumpkin pie spice

½ teaspoon ground cinnamon

½ teaspoon ground ginger

½ teaspoon table salt

3 tablespoons tapioca starch (or cornstarch)

¼ teaspoon freshly ground black pepper

1. Place a rack in the middle of the oven and preheat it to 375°F.

2. To make the crust: In a 9- or 9½-inch pie dish, combine the flour, almond flour, sugar, and salt with a fork. Add the melted butter and mix until fully combined. If your dough looks too wet or won't stick together at this point, stir in a little more flour (up to ¼ cup). Add the milk, 1 tablespoon at a time, mixing between additions. The dough should not stick to your hands, but it should stick together when you pinch some between your fingers.

3. Using your hands, press the dough into the bottom and up the sides of the pan to form the crust. The crust should be ¼ inch thick and as close to the top of the lip on your pie dish as possible. You can crimp the top edge, flatten it, or make designs using a fork or knife.

4. Bake the crust for 6 minutes on the middle rack of the oven, until it is golden brown. Unlike a traditional rolled crust, this won't shrink or puff up as it bakes. Remove the crust from the oven, and reduce the oven temperature to 350°F.

5. To make the filling: In a large bowl, while the crust bakes, whisk the pumpkin, brown sugar, maple syrup, milk, pumpkin pie spice, cinnamon, salt, tapioca starch, and pepper together until smooth. Pour the filling into the parbaked crust (it's okay if the crust is still hot), and smooth the top using a spatula.

6. Bake for 55 to 60 minutes. If the crust starts to brown too quickly, make a foil ring to cover only the crust, leaving the filling exposed. The top of the pie should look evenly golden and should be slightly firm to the touch. It might have a little jiggle at the center, but it will continue to set as it cools.

7. Remove the pie from the oven and place it on a wire rack to cool completely. For best texture and taste, cover the pie with foil and refrigerate overnight before serving.

Per Serving: Calories: 267; Fat: 11g; Saturated Fat: 2g; Cholesterol: 2mg; Carbohydrates: 43g; Fiber: 3g; Protein: 4g; Sodium: 460mg

Pecan Bars

SOY-FREE, CROWD-PLEASER

MAKES: 12 bars | **PREP TIME:** 20 minutes, plus
overnight chilling | **BAKE TIME:** 55 minutes

The pecans in both the crust and topping make these bars reminiscent of pecan pie, but with much less sugar and fuss. If you want to make them even more decadent, try a drizzle of melted chocolate on top.

FOR THE CRUST
Nonstick cooking spray

1 cup gluten-free oats

1 cup unsalted raw pecans

2 tablespoons pure
  maple syrup

2 tablespoons vegan
  brown sugar

¼ teaspoon ground
  cinnamon

4 tablespoons vegan
  butter, melted

⅛ teaspoon table salt

FOR THE FILLING
1 cup full-fat coconut milk

½ cup vegan brown sugar

¼ cup smooth natural
  peanut butter

¼ cup pure maple syrup

1 teaspoon pure
  vanilla extract

3 tablespoons
  tapioca starch

⅛ teaspoon table salt

1 cup roughly
  chopped pecans

1. Preheat the oven to 350°F. Line an 8-inch square baking dish with a piece of parchment paper that overhangs on opposite sides; this sling will help you pull the bars out of the dish after baking. Spray the inside of the dish with a light layer of cooking spray. Set aside.

2. To make the crust: In a blender or food processor, pulse together the oats and pecans until the mixture forms a rough flour. Add the maple syrup, brown sugar, cinnamon, butter, and salt and blend until the dough comes together.

3. Press the dough evenly into the prepared pan. Bake for 20 minutes or until the crust is golden brown and firm to the touch.

4. To make the filling: In a food processor or blender, while the crust bakes, combine the coconut milk, brown sugar, peanut butter, maple syrup, vanilla, tapioca starch, and salt. Puree until smooth, then transfer to a small saucepan. Put the pan over medium-high heat, bring the mixture to a boil, then reduce the heat to medium and simmer for 5 minutes. The filling should be noticeably thicker, but it will become even thicker as it cools.

5. Pour the filling over the baked crust, sprinkle the pecans evenly over top, and bake for 30 minutes.

6. Remove the pan from the oven. Let cool on a wire rack for 30 minutes, then cover and refrigerate overnight. Using the parchment "handles," lift the pecan bars out of the dish and onto a plate or cutting board. Cut into squares and enjoy!

Per Serving (1 bar): Calories: 325; Fat: 23g; Saturated Fat: 6g; Cholesterol: 0mg; Carbohydrates: 28g; Fiber: 3g; Protein: 5g; Sodium: 61mg

Avocado Brownies

SERVES: 8 | **PREP TIME:** 15 minutes | **BAKE TIME:** 30 minutes

These brownies are fudgy, chocolatey, and easy to make. An avocado might seem like an odd ingredient for brownies, but the avocado's naturally high fat content makes these brownies gooey and decadent without added oil or butter. Plus, if anyone questions you about eating brownies, you can just tell them that they're good for you!

Nonstick cooking spray

½ cup firm silken tofu

1 medium, ripe Hass avocado, pitted and mashed (roughly ¾ cup)

¼ cup safflower or avocado oil

¼ cup smooth natural peanut butter (or sunflower seed butter to make it nut-free)

½ teaspoon baking soda

¼ teaspoon table salt

⅓ cup vegan brown sugar

⅓ cup unsweetened cocoa powder

1 teaspoon pure vanilla extract

3 tablespoons tapioca starch

½ cup vegan dark chocolate chips, plus more for sprinkling

Chopped nuts for sprinkling (optional)

1. Preheat the oven to 350°F. Line an 8-inch square baking dish with a piece of parchment paper that overhangs on opposite sides; this sling will help you pull the bars out of the dish after baking. Spray the inside of the dish with a light layer of cooking spray. Set aside.

2. In a food processor, combine the tofu, avocado, oil, peanut butter, baking soda, salt, brown sugar, cocoa powder, vanilla, tapioca starch, and chocolate. Process until just smooth. Scrape down the sides and pulse once or twice to combine.

3. Transfer the batter to the prepared baking dish and smooth the top. Top the batter with more chocolate chips and the nuts, if desired.

4. Bake for 30 minutes, until the edges separate from the sides of the dish. Remove from the oven and let cool on a wire rack for 15 minutes.

5. Gently pull the brownies out of the pan using the parchment paper sling. Transfer to a cutting board and cut into 8 pieces.

6. Enjoy immediately, or refrigerate the brownies overnight (they're even better after chilling). Store in an airtight container in the refrigerator for up to 1 week.

Per Serving (1 brownie): Calories: 271; Fat: 20g; Saturated Fat: 5g; Cholesterol: 0mg; Carbohydrates: 22g; Fiber: 5g; Protein: 5g; Sodium: 160mg

Apple Cider Muffins

NUT-FREE, SOY-FREE, 30 MINUTES, CROWD-PLEASER

MAKES: 12 muffins | **PREP TIME:** 15 minutes | **BAKE TIME:** 14 minutes

These muffins will taste as good as they make your house smell. They are quick to make, and delicious as either a muffin or a cupcake with frosting on top. The pumpkin pie spice gives it that cozy autumnal feel.

Nonstick cooking spray

2 cups 1:1 all-purpose gluten-free flour, homemade (page 206) or store-bought

½ cup vegan sugar

1 teaspoon baking soda

1 teaspoon baking powder

1 teaspoon pumpkin pie spice

¼ teaspoon table salt

1 cup apple cider (not vinegar)

2 tablespoons avocado oil or melted vegan butter

¼ cup no-added-sugar applesauce

½ cup unsweetened gluten-free nondairy milk, homemade (page 218) or store-bought

1 teaspoon pure vanilla extract

---

1. Preheat the oven to 350°F. Spray a muffin pan with cooking spray, or line the cups with parchment liners. Set aside.

2. In a medium mixing bowl, whisk together the flour, sugar, baking soda, baking powder, pumpkin pie spice, and salt.

3. In a separate bowl, mix the apple cider, oil, applesauce, milk, and vanilla. Combine half of the wet ingredients into the dry, fold to mix, then fold in the remaining wet ingredients.

4. Fill each muffin mold about three-quarters full. Bake for 12 to 14 minutes, until the tops are golden brown. Let cool for 1 minute in the pan, then cool the muffins completely on a wire rack.

CHANGE IT UP: For a bit of texture, add ½ cup chopped pecans or walnuts with the final addition of the wet ingredients. You can also add in a finely diced green apple at that stage for even more apple flavor.

Per Serving (1 muffin): Calories: 168; Fat: 3g; Saturated Fat: 1g; Cholesterol: 1mg; Carbohydrates: 33g; Fiber: 1g; Protein: 2g; Sodium: 160mg

Drop Biscuits

ESSENTIAL RECIPE, NUT-FREE, SOY-FREE, 30 MINUTES, CROWD-PLEASER

MAKES: 12 biscuits | **PREP TIME:** 15 minutes | **BAKE TIME:** 15 minutes

Biscuits can be served as a breakfast base, a dessert topped with fresh fruit, or as a sophisticated party side with some herbs and spices stirred in. If you are new to baking, biscuits are a great way to start. These drop biscuits are light and fluffy with a little crunch to the edges, and you don't need to roll out dough.

---

1 cup unsweetened gluten-free nondairy milk, homemade (page 218) or store-bought

1 teaspoon apple cider vinegar

1½ 1:1 all-purpose gluten-free flour, homemade (page 206) or store-bought

½ cup cornstarch

1 tablespoon baking powder

¼ teaspoon baking soda

½ teaspoon table salt

6 tablespoons cold vegan butter

---

1. Preheat the oven to 425°F. Line a rimmed baking sheet with parchment and set aside.

2. In a small bowl or measuring cup, mix together the milk and vinegar. Set aside.

3. In a large bowl, whisk together the flour, cornstarch, baking powder, baking soda, and salt. Slice the cold butter directly into the flour mixture in ¼-inch or smaller pieces, then use a pastry cutter or 2 forks to cut the butter into the dry mixture until it is the size of small peas.

4. Using a spatula, fold the milk mixture into the flour mixture until no dry spots remain. Your dough should be fairly wet and sticky, but still thick.

5. Scoop ¼-cup mounds of dough onto the prepared baking sheet, leaving 1 inch or more space between the biscuits.

6. Bake for 12 to 15 minutes, until the tops and edges are golden brown. Let them sit for 5 minutes before serving. Store in an airtight container on the counter for up to 5 days, or freeze for longer storage.

Per Serving (1 biscuit): Calories: 151; Fat: 6g; Saturated Fat: 1g; Cholesterol: 0mg; Carbohydrates: 22g; Fiber: 1g; Protein: 2g; Sodium: 136mg

Salted Walnut-Maple Brittle

SOY-FREE, 30 MINUTES, CROWD-PLEASER

SERVES: 8 | **PREP TIME:** 5 minutes | **COOK TIME:** 15 to 20 minutes

Sweet, crunchy, salty, and nutty: If it sounds delicious, that's because it is. You will need a candy thermometer for this recipe because it's easy to burn. But never fear, candy making is easier than you might think, and this recipe may start you on a whole new candy-making journey.

---

2 cups coarsely chopped walnuts

¼ cup pure maple syrup

1 cup vegan sugar

1 cup vegan butter, cut into pieces

¼ cup water

Flaky salt or kosher salt

---

1. Heat a medium skillet over medium-high heat. Add the walnuts and cook, stirring constantly, until the nuts are fragrant and starting to brown. Remove the skillet from the heat and transfer the nuts to a plate or bowl to cool. Set aside.

2. Line a large rimmed baking sheet with parchment paper.

3. Heat a heavy-bottomed medium pot over medium heat. Pour in the maple syrup, sugar, butter, and water; stir until the sugar and butter have melted and the mixture is creamy. Once the mixture starts to bubble, stop stirring. Note: Do not lick your spoon or touch the mixture at any stage of this recipe. Hot sugar can cause very bad burns.

4. Attach a candy thermometer to the pot and continue to gently boil until the candy thermometer reaches 300°F (a.k.a. "hard crack" stage) and is thick, foamy, fully bubbling, and lightly golden, 5 to 10 minutes. Remove from the heat and immediately stir in the walnuts.

5. Quickly but carefully, pour the hot brittle mixture onto the prepared baking sheet. Use a heatproof spoon to spread it out in a thin, even layer. Sprinkle the top with a little salt to taste.

6. Allow the brittle to cool completely on the baking sheet. Break it into large pieces, and store the brittle in an airtight container on the counter for up to 2 weeks. If you are making this ahead, freeze the brittle instead of refrigerating it to keep it crispy.

TECHNIQUE TIP: Candy making is a simple process that primarily involves heating sugar to a certain temperature. You will need a candy thermometer to help you reach the precise candy stages. You can find candy thermometers at most grocery stores, online, or at many big box stores for under $10.

Per Serving: Calories: 516; Fat: 42g; Saturated Fat: 6g; Cholesterol: 0mg; Carbohydrates: 36g; Fiber: 2g; Protein: 5g; Sodium: 29mg

Matcha Shortbread

NUT-FREE, SOY-FREE, CROWD-PLEASER

MAKES: 24 cookies | **PREP TIME:** 30 minutes, plus 2 hours chilling time | **BAKE TIME:** 15 minutes

Sweet sorghum flour enhances the slightly bitter, earthy flavor of matcha, Japanese green tea powder. The taste is unique and pleasing, and the bright green color makes it a fun treat. Pro tip: elevate these vibrant green cookies by dipping them in melted chocolate.

1½ cups 1:1 all-purpose gluten-free flour, homemade (page 206) or store-bought

½ cup sweet sorghum flour

2½ tablespoons matcha powder

¾ cup vegan butter, room temperature

1 cup vegan sugar

⅛ teaspoon kosher salt

2 tablespoons no-added-sugar applesauce

---

1. In a large bowl, whisk together the flours and matcha powder. For even better results, sift the flour or use a fine-mesh strainer.

2. In a stand mixer or with a hand mixer and a bowl, beat the softened butter until cremy, scrape the sides of the bowl, then beat in the sugar and salt. Scrape the sides and beat in the applesauce.

3. Using a heavy wooden spoon, mix the flour into the butter mixture until fully combined. Transfer the dough to your counter and divide the dough in half. Shape the dough into a cylinder that is 2 inches thick and 6 inches long. Wrap the dough in plastic and refrigerate for at least 2 hours.

4. Preheat the oven to 350ºF. Line a large rimmed baking sheet with parchment paper.

5. Unwrap the dough cylinders and cut them into ½-inch-thick pieces. Place the cut pieces of dough on the prepared baking sheet with 2 inches of space between them.

6. Bake for 15 minutes or until the edges of the cookies have turned a golden brown.

7. Remove the baking sheet from the oven, let the cookies cool on the sheet for 5 minutes, then transfer them to a wire rack to cool completely. Store in an airtight container on the counter for up to a week, or freeze the cookies in an airtight container for longer storage.

TECHNIQUE TIP: For beautifully round cookies, consider chilling the dough in a bed of rice so they keep their even shape. Pour rice into a baking dish, place the plastic-wrapped dough on top, gently nestle the dough into the rice, and then refrigerate.

Per Serving (1 cookie): Calories: 128; Fat: 6g; Saturated Fat: 1g; Cholesterol: 0mg; Carbohydrates: 18g; Fiber: 1g; Protein: 1g; Sodium: 16mg

Peach and Blueberry Galette

SOY-FREE, CROWD-PLEASER

SERVES: 8 | **PREP TIME:** 30 minutes, plus 1 hour chilling time | **BAKE TIME:** 35 minutes

A galette is a free-form pie that you can master on your first try; there's a much bigger margin of error than with a regular pie! Their rustic look is what makes them aesthetically pleasing, and you don't even need a pie dish. Whether you make it for a summer potluck or a holiday party, this recipe will have everyone asking for seconds.

FOR THE CRUST

1 tablespoon ground flaxseed

3 tablespoons cold water

1½ cups almond flour

½ cup tapioca starch

½ teaspoon xanthan gum

1 tablespoon vegan sugar

¼ teaspoon kosher salt

6 tablespoons cold vegan butter

FOR THE FILLING

1 cup fresh blueberries

1 tablespoon freshly squeezed lemon juice

1 tablespoon lemon zest

2 tablespoons pure maple syrup

1 teaspoon pure vanilla extract

2 teaspoons tapioca starch

¼ teaspoon ground cinnamon

2 large peaches, pitted and cut into ¼-inch-thick slices

FOR FINISHING THE PIE

1 tablespoon aquafaba, liquid from chickpea can

¼ teaspoon ground cinnamon

1 tablespoon sugar

1. To make the crust: In a small bowl, whisk together the ground flaxseed and water. Set aside to thicken.

2. In a food processor, combine the almond flour, tapioca starch, xanthan gum, sugar, and salt. Pulse 2 or 3 times to mix. Cut in ¼-inch pieces of cold butter and add to the food processor. Process for 5 seconds to break the butter into small pieces. You can also use a pastry cutter for this step.

3. Pour in the soaked flaxseed and pulse 2 or 3 times, until the dough comes together. Turn the dough onto a piece of plastic wrap, then press it into a

1-inch-thick disk, roughly 6 inches in diameter. Wrap the disk in plastic and refrigerate it for at least 1 hour or up to overnight. Leave it in the refrigerator until you're ready to build your pie.

4. Preheat the oven to 375°F.

5. To make the filling: In a medium bowl, stir together the blueberries, lemon juice and zest, maple syrup, vanilla, tapioca starch, and cinnamon. Toss in the sliced peaches.

6. Place a piece of parchment paper on your work surface. Unwrap the dough and place it on the parchment paper. Place another piece of parchment paper on top and roll the dough until it is 10 inches in diameter. Remove the parchment paper from the top. Transfer the dough on the parchment to a large rimmed baking sheet.

7. Place the filling in the middle of the dough circle, leaving a 2-inch margin of empty dough around the edge.

8. Starting on one side, fold the dough edge toward the middle and work your way around the dough circle while creasing the dough with your fingers. Use the parchment paper under the dough to help fold it so that it doesn't crack or break.

9. To finish the pie: Brush the pie crust with the aquafaba, then sprinkle the crust with the cinnamon and sugar.

10. Bake for 30 to 35 minutes, until the crust is golden brown and the blueberries have burst. Let cool for 10 minutes before serving.

TECHNIQUE TIP: A galette gets its beauty from the exposed filling and variety of colors. You can get creative with how you arrange your peach slices and blueberries. Stand the peach slices on their cut edges so that the skin is showing, then push them to their side slightly, like fallen dominos. It is a simple technique but very beautiful.

Per Serving: Calories: 239; Fat: 17g; Saturated Fat: 2g; Cholesterol: 0mg; Carbohydrates: 21g; Fiber: 3g; Protein: 4g; Sodium: 62mg

Snickerdoodle Bundt Cake

NUT-FREE, SOY-FREE, CROWD-PLEASER

SERVES: 12 | **PREP TIME:** 20 minutes | **BAKE TIME:** 50 minutes

Bundt cakes look beautiful, with no decorating required, because the stunning design comes from the pan. The center hole of these rich, moist cakes ensures that the thick batter cooks evenly. Plus, with more surface area, you get more of the caramelized edge.

Nonstick cooking spray

1¼ cups vegan granulated sugar, divided

2½ teaspoons ground cinnamon, divided

2¼ cups 1:1 all-purpose gluten-free flour, homemade (page 206) or store-bought

1 teaspoon baking powder

½ teaspoon baking soda

½ teaspoon cream of tartar

¼ teaspoon ground nutmeg

½ teaspoon table salt

¾ cup unsalted vegan butter, at room temperature

½ cup vegan brown sugar

¾ cup no-added-sugar applesauce

1 teaspoon pure vanilla extract

1 cup full-fat coconut milk

---

1. Preheat the oven to 350°F. Spray a 12-cup Bundt pan liberally with cooking spray. Set aside.

2. In a small bowl, mix ½ cup sugar with 1 teaspoon cinnamon. Sprinkle half of the cinnamon sugar into the prepared pan, making sure to coat the sides and center. Pat the pan so that there aren't areas with excess cinnamon sugar. This will form a delicious crust on the baked cake.

3. In a medium bowl, whisk together the flour, baking powder, baking soda, cream of tartar, ground nutmeg, salt, and remaining 1½ teaspoons cinnamon.

4. Using a stand mixer or hand mixer and bowl, cream together the butter, brown sugar, and remaining ¾ cup of granulated sugar. The sugar should be fully incorporated into the butter, and the mixture should be more fluffy than oily looking. Beat in the applesauce until fully combined, scraping the sides once or twice. Add the vanilla and mix to combine.

5. Continue to use your mixer on low, or use a heavy spoon to fold in half of the flour mixture, then half of the coconut milk. Fold in the remaining flour, then the rest of the coconut milk, stirring just until the batter is free of dry spots.

6. Pour half of the batter into the prepared pan. Sprinkle the remaining cinnamon-sugar mixture over the batter, and use a knife to swirl it. Top with the rest of the batter and use the knife to smooth the top.

7. Bake for 40 to 50 minutes or until a cake tester or toothpick inserted in the center comes out clean.

8. Remove the pan from the oven, place it on a wire rack, and let it cool for 30 minutes. Then, carefully invert the cake onto the wire rack to finish cooling. The cinnamon sugar from the pan will harden as the cake cools, forming a crunchy exterior, just like a snickerdoodle cookie!

TECHNIQUE TIP: The beauty of a Bundt cake is in the pan, but that also means lots of nooks and crannies for batter to get trapped in. Make sure to use a spray oil for a Bundt pan if it has an intricate design. If your cake does not easily release from the pan, place it on a warm stove burner for a few minutes, metal-side down, dip it in a bowl of warm water for 1 minute, then try again.

Per Serving: Calories: 371; Fat: 16g; Saturated Fat: 6g; Cholesterol: 0mg; Carbohydrates: 56g; Fiber: 2g; Protein: 3g; Sodium: 162mg

No-Bake Caramel Brownie Bars

SOY-FREE, 30 MINUTES, CROWD-PLEASER

MAKES: 16 brownie bars | **PREP TIME:** 30 minutes, plus
35 minutes freezing time

This fudgy, decadent dessert bar combines raw nuts and dates to create a chewy brownie layer. And as if that's not enough, this recipe adds a gooey caramel layer made with peanut butter and a melted chocolate layer on top of that. Although you'll want to keep them all to yourself for a late-night grab, these bars make a great dessert to bring to a gathering.

FOR THE BROWNIE LAYER
Nonstick cooking spray

1 cup ground flaxseed

½ cup unsweetened
   cocoa powder

⅛ teaspoon kosher salt

1½ cups pitted
   Medjool dates

2 teaspoon pure
   vanilla extract

Pure maple syrup,
   as needed

1 cup sliced almonds

FOR THE CARAMEL LAYER
¼ cup pure maple syrup

⅓ cup full-fat canned
   coconut milk

¼ cup coconut sugar or
   vegan brown sugar

3 tablespoons smooth
   natural peanut butter

Pinch sea salt

FOR THE CHOCOLATE LAYER
1 cup vegan chocolate chips

2 teaspoons coconut oil

1. To make the brownie layer: Line an 8-inch square baking dish with a piece of parchment paper that overhangs on opposite sides; this sling will help you pull the bars out of the dish after baking. Spray the inside of the dish with a light layer of cooking spray. Set aside.

2. In a food processor, combine the ground flaxseed, cocoa powder, salt, dates, and vanilla. Process until the dough starts to stick together, which can take several minutes. If it seems too dry, add a teaspoon at a time of pure maple syrup. Add the sliced almonds and pulse to combine.

3. Scrape the brownie dough into the prepared baking dish, and press it to the edges so it forms an even layer. Set aside.

4. To make the caramel layer: In a medium saucepan, mix together the maple syrup, coconut milk, sugar, peanut butter, and salt and bring to a boil. Reduce the heat to a simmer and cook for 15 minutes, stirring frequently at first and then continuously in the final 5 minutes.

5. Pour the caramel over the brownie layer, and place the dish in the freezer for 30 minutes.

6. To make the chocolate layer: Before removing the dish from the freezer, make the chocolate layer. Melt the chocolate and coconut oil in the microwave, heating for 30 seconds at a time and mixing in between, or use a double boiler.

7. Pour the chocolate over the chilled caramel layer, then freeze for a final 5 minutes.

8. To serve, use the parchment "handles" to lift the brownie out of the dish and onto a plate or cutting board. Cut with a hot knife. Store in an airtight container in the refrigerator, or freeze for longer storage.

Per Serving (1 brownie bar): Calories: 222; Fat: 13g; Saturated Fat: 4g; Cholesterol: 0mg; Carbohydrates: 26g; Fiber: 6g; Protein: 5g; Sodium: 31mg

Orange-Vanilla Pound Cake

SERVES: 12 | **PREP TIME:** 15 minutes | **BAKE TIME:** 1 hour

Pound cake gets its name from the proportions in the original, early-1700s version of the recipe, which called for one pound each of butter, sugar, eggs, and flour (no leavener). The result was a dense and moist cake. This pound cake is fragrant with orange zest and vanilla, and although it is moist, it's a little airier than its leaden predecessor.

Nonstick cooking spray

3 cups 1:1 all-purpose gluten-free flour, homemade (page 206) or store-bought, plus more for dusting the pan

2 cups vegan sugar

1 cup vegan butter, melted

1 cup no-added-sugar applesauce

1 tablespoon pure vanilla extract

3 tablespoons freshly squeezed orange juice (from 1 orange)

2 teaspoons baking powder

1 tablespoon orange zest

½ teaspoon kosher salt

1 cup unsweetened gluten-free nondairy milk, homemade (page 218) or store-bought

1. Preheat the oven to 350°F. Spray a 12-cup Bundt pan with a light layer of cooking spray. Sprinkle a little flour into the pan, and tap and roll the pan around to coat the pan with flour (see Technique Tip).

2. In a medium bowl, use a whisk or handheld mixer to beat the sugar and butter together until creamy. Mix in the applesauce, ¼ cup at a time, then mix in the vanilla and orange juice. The wet ingredients might look curdled, but that is normal.

3. In a separate large bowl, whisk together the flour, baking powder, orange zest, and salt. Stir half of the dry mixture into the wet ingredients, add half of the milk, and repeat until all the flour mixture and milk are incorporated.

4. Pour the batter into the prepared pan. Bake for 50 to 60 minutes or until a toothpick inserted in the center comes out clean. Remove the pan from the oven and place it on a wire rack to cool for 10 minutes. Carefully invert the pan onto the wire rack and let the cake cool completely.

5. Serve as is, or dust with a light layer of powdered sugar.

TECHNIQUE TIP: The light dusting of flour or sugar in a pan for cake recipes actually serves a purpose that isn't about making the pan nonstick. That light layer of flour helps the batter cling to the sides of the pan as it rises, which ensures an even and higher rise.

Per Serving: Calories: 433; Fat: 16g; Saturated Fat: 3g; Cholesterol: 2mg; Carbohydrates: 69g; Fiber: 1g; Protein: 3g; Sodium: 75mg

Seeded Sandwich Bread

ESSENTIAL RECIPE, SOY-FREE, CROWD-PLEASER

MAKES: 1 loaf | **PREP TIME:** 20 minutes, plus 1 to 1½ hours rising time
and 1 hour cooling time | **BAKE TIME:** 55 minutes

Sandwiches are a lunch or quick dinner staple, but good gluten-free and vegan sandwich bread is a rarity at most grocery stores. If you can find it, it is usually expensive and has a long list of ingredients. This recipe gives you a tasty, hearty, crusty bread that is filled with seeds and nuts that offer both texture and plant-based nutrients.

¼ cup ground flaxseed

½ cup water

3 cups 1:1 all-purpose gluten-free flour, homemade (page 206) or store-bought

½ teaspoon xanthan gum

¼ cup pumpkin seeds

¼ cup gluten-free oats

¼ cup chopped walnuts, pecans, or sliced almonds

1 tablespoon chia seeds

1½ teaspoons instant dry yeast (see Ingredient Smarts tip)

1 teaspoon table salt

¾ cup unsweetened gluten-free nondairy milk, homemade (page 218) or store-bought, warmed to no more than 100°F

2 tablespoons molasses (not blackstrap)

¼ cup avocado or safflower oil

Nonstick cooking spray

1. In a small bowl, mix together the ground flaxseed and water. Set aside.

2. In the bowl of a stand mixer or large bowl, combine the flour, xanthan gum, pumpkin seeds, oats, nuts, chia seeds, yeast, and salt. Mix to disperse the yeast throughout the flour mixture.

3. In a measuring cup or small bowl, whisk together the milk, molasses, oil, and soaked flaxseed. Pour the wet ingredients into the dry ingredients while mixing on low speed or with a heavy spoon. If the dough looks dry, add a tablespoon of water or milk.

4. Continue to mix the dough for 3 to 5 minutes until it looks smooth. Cover the bowl and let the dough rise for 30 minutes.

5. Lightly spray a loaf pan with cooking spray. Scoop the dough into the pan. Using a spatula or your wet fingers, press the dough into the pan and shape it in the pan by pressing the sides down in the pan to make a dome on the top or a loaf shape. Spray the top with cooking spray and cover with plastic wrap.

6. Set the bread in a warm place to rise for 30 to 60 minutes. The dome of the dough should extend just past the rim of the pan. Do not let it rise longer than 1 hour.

7. Place a rack in the middle of the oven and preheat it to 350°F.

8. Remove the plastic wrap and place the bread on the middle rack of the oven. Bake for 45 to 55 minutes, until the top is evenly golden brown and the internal temperature is over 195°F.

9. Remove the bread from the oven and let it cool on a wire rack for 5 minutes. Then, turn it on its side to gently remove it from the pan, and place the bread directly on the wire rack. Allow it to cool completely, about 1 hour, before slicing. The internal heat continues to cook the bread after it's out of the oven.

10. Store the bread tightly wrapped in plastic at room temperature for 1 day, or slice it and freeze in an airtight container for longer storage.

CHANGE IT UP: You can modify this recipe by changing the seeds, nuts, and oats, as long as the total equals ¾ cup. Also, you can swap the molasses for an equal amount of pure maple syrup, but the molasses helps the dough stay moist.

INGREDIENT SMARTS: Dry instant yeast and dry active yeast are two different styles of yeast for baking. Dry active yeast needs to be proofed first by mixing it with a small amount of water and sugar so that the coating on the yeast granules can dissolve, allowing the living yeast to work. If a recipe calls for instant yeast, it shouldn't be substituted with dry active yeast unless you are comfortable with yeast baking.

Per Serving (1/12 loaf): Calories: 262; Fat: 10g; Saturated Fat: 1g; Cholesterol: 1mg; Carbohydrates: 39g; Fiber: 3g; Protein: 5g; Sodium: 210mg

Burger Buns

ESSENTIAL RECIPE, NUT-FREE, SOY-FREE, CROWD-PLEASER

MAKES: 8 buns | **PREP TIME:** 20 minutes, plus 1½ hours rising time and 15 to 30 minutes chilling time | **BAKE TIME:** 18 minutes

These buns are used often throughout this cookbook for croutons, hoagies, and, well, burgers. It can be very challenging to find gluten-free and vegan burger buns in most grocery stores, and if you do find them, there's usually a limited selection. Trust me: The lengthy ingredient list will be worth it. This recipe gives you a solid base for even the juiciest of vegan burgers.

1 tablespoon ground flaxseed

2 tablespoons, plus 1 cup warm water, divided

½ cup unsweetened gluten-free nondairy milk, homemade (page 218) or store-bought

1 teaspoon apple cider vinegar

3¼ cups 1:1 all-purpose gluten-free flour, homemade (page 206) or store-bought, plus more for work surface and kneading

½ teaspoon xanthan gum

1 tablespoon instant dry yeast

¼ teaspoon cream of tartar

¼ teaspoon baking soda

1 tablespoon vegan light brown sugar

1 teaspoon kosher salt

2 tablespoons vegan butter, at room temperature

Nonstick cooking spray

Oil or aquafaba (canned chickpea liquid), for brushing

1. In a small bowl, mix the ground flaxseed and 2 tablespoons water. In a separate measuring cup or bowl, mix together the milk and vinegar. Set both of these aside while you prepare the remaining ingredients.

2. In a large bowl or the bowl of a stand mixer, add the flour, xanthan gum, yeast, cream of tartar, baking soda, sugar, and salt. Mix to fully combine the dry ingredients using a whisk or the paddle attachment.

3. Add the butter, soaked flaxseed, 1 cup of water, and the milk mixture from step 1, and mix with a heavy spoon or paddle attachment until thick and smooth.

4. Transfer the dough to a lightly oiled bowl and cover. Let rise for an hour until the dough has nearly doubled in size.

5. Once the dough has risen, transfer the covered bowl to the refrigerator to chill for 15 to 30 minutes. This makes it easier to handle.

6. Turn the dough out on a lightly floured work surface, sprinkle the top with additional flour. Knead the dough a little, using more flour as needed, until it is smooth. Divide the dough in half, place one half back in the oiled bowl, and cover.

7. Divide the dough half into four equal parts. Shape each part into a domed roll by pinching the sides and pulling them underneath, then rolling it with the side of your palm gently pressed against the surface and guiding it with your fingertips into a round. Sprinkle the dough with more flour and press it into a 4-inch disk that is about ¾-inch thick. Transfer the shaped buns to a large, parchment-lined rimmed baking sheet. Repeat with the other half of the dough to make a total of 8 shaped buns.

8. Spray the tops with a light layer of cooking spray. Cover the pans with plastic wrap and let the buns rise at room temperature for 30 minutes.

9. Preheat the oven to 400°F.

10. Brush the tops with oil or aquafaba, remove the plastic covering, and bake for 15 to 18 minutes, rotating the pans halfway. The tops should be a pale brown with an internal temperature of at least 195°F. Remove the buns from the oven and let them cool completely on a wire rack. Store in an airtight container on the counter for 1 day or slice and freeze the buns in an airtight container for longer storage.

CHANGE IT UP: To turn these into hoagies or hot dog buns, shape them by rolling the dough back and forth on your counter instead of balling it up. If you're making hot dog buns, divide the dough into 8 pieces; if you're making hoagie rolls, divide the dough into 6 pieces.

If you want sesame seed buns, brush a mixture of 1 teaspoon of cornstarch and 1 tablespoon of aquafaba on the dough, and then sprinkle seeds on top before baking.

Per Serving (1 bun): Calories: 282; Fat: 5g; Saturated Fat: 1g; Cholesterol: 1mg; Carbohydrates: 54g; Fiber: 2g; Protein: 5g; Sodium: 254mg

CHAPTER 9

Basics

Homemade All-Purpose 1:1 Gluten-Free Flour Blend

ESSENTIAL RECIPE, NUT-FREE, SOY-FREE, 30 MINUTES

MAKES: 9 cups, or roughly 2½ pounds | **PREP TIME:** 15 minutes

There are more gluten-free flour blends in grocery stores these days, but each brand has its own combination of flours, which can affect flavor and texture. This recipe offers a 1:1 all-purpose gluten-free flour blend that can be used for any of the recipes in this book, as well as any of your own creations. The bonus is that you can change the balance of flours in order to give your baked good a different flavor or color (see the Ingredient Smarts tip below).

4½ cups white rice flour	1½ cups potato starch	¾ cup sorghum flour
1½ cups brown rice flour	¾ cup tapioca starch	1 tablespoon xanthan gum

---

1. In a large bowl, or in a stand mixer or food processor, combine the white rice flour, brown rice flour, potato starch, tapioca starch, sorghum flower, and xanthan gum, and whisk or process to combine evenly.

2. Store in an airtight container away from sunlight for up to 3 months.

INGREDIENT SMARTS: Xanthan gum acts as a binding agent, similar to the role of gluten in wheat doughs. This flour blend works well for softer doughs like a cake, muffin, or quick bread. Some baked goods, like pizza or bread dough, are meant to be tougher, so they'll require a little more xanthan gum: Add 1 additional teaspoon of xanthan gum per cup of flour.

Per Serving (¼ cup): Calories: 139; Fat: 0g; Saturated Fat: 0g; Cholesterol: 0mg; Carbohydrates: 31g; Fiber: 1g; Protein: 2g; Sodium: 4mg

BBQ Sauce

ESSENTIAL RECIPE, NUT-FREE, SOY-FREE, 30 MINUTES

MAKES: 1 pint | **PREP TIME:** 12 minutes | **COOK TIME:** 18 minutes

Bottled barbecue sauce is notorious for hiding gluten and non-vegan ingredients, and most store-bought versions are loaded with sugar. Making your own sauce is affordable, easy, quick, and ingredient-transparent.

---

1 cup chopped yellow onion

¼ cup apple cider vinegar

4 garlic cloves, chopped

1 (6-ounce) can tomato paste

½ cup vegan brown sugar

½ teaspoon kosher salt

½ teaspoon freshly ground black pepper

1 tablespoon liquid smoke

2 tablespoons vegan Worcestershire sauce

1 teaspoon hot sauce of choice

1 cup Sun-Dried-Tomato Ketchup (page 216) or store-bought gluten-free ketchup

1½ cups water

---

1. In a small pot over medium heat, cook the onion, vinegar, and garlic for 5 minutes, stirring occasionally, until the onion is translucent. Stir in the tomato paste, brown sugar, salt, and pepper. Cook for 3 minutes, stirring constantly, then add the liquid smoke, Worcestershire sauce, hot sauce, ketchup, and water; simmer for 10 minutes or until the sauce is thick.

2. Using an immersion blender or upright blender, blend until smooth. Store in the refrigerator in an airtight container, like a mason jar, for up to 3 weeks.

Per Serving (2 tablespoons): Calories: 58; Fat: 0g; Saturated Fat: 0g; Cholesterol: 0mg; Carbohydrates: 15g; Fiber: 1g; Protein: 1g; Sodium: 224mg

Hummus

ESSENTIAL RECIPE, NUT-FREE, SOY-FREE, 30 MINUTES,
CROWD-PLEASER, WHOLE-FOOD PLANT-BASED

MAKES: 1⅓ cups | **PREP TIME:** 20 minutes

Homemade hummus is better than store-bought versions because you know the exact ingredients and the exact freshness. This basic recipe reveals the secret to restaurant-style, creamy hummus at home, plus a couple of ideas for savory and dessert variations.

---

1 (15-ounce) can chickpeas (reserve 3 tablespoons aquafaba, liquid from the can; drain the rest)

¼ cup tahini

1 tablespoon freshly squeezed lemon juice

1 tablespoon extra-virgin olive oil

½ teaspoon ground cumin

1 garlic clove, peeled and crushed

½ teaspoon kosher salt

---

1. In a large bowl, combine the chickpeas and enough water to cover them by 4 inches. Gently rub the chickpeas between your hands to remove the outer layers or skins, and stir the chickpeas in the bowl to get the peels to float to the top. Using your hand, scoop the peels off the water's surface; add more water if necessary, and repeat until you've removed as many peels as possible. This process makes the hummus extra velvety. Pour the peeled chickpeas into a colander to drain, then set them aside.

2. In a food processor or high-speed blender, combine the reserved 3 tablespoons of aquafaba, tahini, lemon juice, and oil, and process for 2 minutes. This step emulsifies the liquids and whips the aquafaba, which will make your hummus even smoother and lighter.

3. Add the cumin, garlic, and salt, and puree for 1 minute. Finally, add the chickpeas and blend for 2 to 3 minutes or until the hummus is smooth, scraping down the sides as necessary.

4. Serve immediately or refrigerate in an airtight container for up to 2 weeks.

CHANGE IT UP: There are so many creative variations on hummus; here are a few of my favorites:

Beet and Herb Hummus: Add ½ cup cubed and boiled beets with the chickpeas and replace the cumin with ½ teaspoon dried thyme and ½ teaspoon dried rosemary.

Chocolate Dessert Hummus: In step 2, replace the tahini with peanut or almond butter and add ¼ cup unsweetened cocoa powder, 1 tablespoon pure maple syrup, and 1 teaspoon pure vanilla extract. Omit the garlic, lemon juice, oil and cumin.

Carrot Cake Hummus: Replace the tahini with almond or cashew butter, omit the garlic and cumin, and replace the olive oil with avocado or safflower oil. Add 1 tablespoon vegan brown sugar, 1 teaspoon ground cinnamon, ¼ teaspoon ground ginger, and ¼ teaspoon ground nutmeg. After processing, use a spoon to stir in ½ cup grated carrot and ¼ cup chopped walnuts or pecans.

Per Serving (⅓ cup): Calories: 201; Fat: 13g; Saturated Fat: 2g; Cholesterol: 0mg; Carbohydrates: 17g; Fiber: 5g; Protein: 7g; Sodium: 342mg

Sunflower Seed Cheese Sauce

ESSENTIAL RECIPE, NUT-FREE, SOY-FREE, CROWD-PLEASER,
WHOLE-FOOD PLANT-BASED

MAKES: 4 cups | **PREP TIME:** 10 minutes | **COOK TIME:** 25 minutes

This cheese sauce can be used for many recipes, like Hasselback Potatoes (page 109) and, of course, Chili Mac and Cheese (page 154). The key to success is to use raw sunflower seeds, because the roasted ones won't break down into a smooth sauce. However, you can swap in raw cashews for the sunflower seeds for an even creamier sauce.

---

1 cup raw sunflower seeds

1 medium russet potato, peeled and cubed

2 medium carrots, peeled and cubed

1 medium yellow onion, chopped

3 garlic cloves, roughly chopped

½ cup nutritional yeast

2 tablespoons white miso paste

2 cups unsweetened gluten-free nondairy milk, homemade (page 218) or store-bought

1 tablespoon tapioca starch

---

1. In a large pot, combine the sunflower seeds, potato, carrot, onion, and garlic, and add enough water to cover the ingredients by 2 inches. Bring to a boil, reduce to a simmer and partially cover the pot. Cook for 20 minutes.

2. Drain the sunflower seed mixture into a colander. Rinse out the pot with cool water to remove any starchy foam (no need to wash the pot).

3. Transfer the sunflower seed mixture to a blender or food processor. Add the nutritional yeast, miso, milk, and tapioca starch and process until smooth. Scrape the sides as necessary.

4. Return the pureed mixture to the large pot over medium heat, and bring it to a simmer, roughly 3 minutes, while stirring. Use the sauce immediately, or store it in the refrigerator in an airtight container for up to 2 weeks.

Per Serving (¼ cup): Calories: 97; Fat: 5g; Saturated Fat: 0g; Cholesterol: 0mg; Carbohydrates: 10g; Fiber: 2g; Protein: 5g; Sodium: 289mg

Cashew Ranch Dressing

SOY-FREE, CROWD-PLEASER, WHOLE-FOOD PLANT-BASED

MAKES: 2 cups | **PREP TIME:** 15 minutes, plus
1 hour chilling time | **COOK TIME:** 20 minutes

Ranch dressing is an iconic salad dressing, and it makes a great dip for just about anything. With this nut-based version, you get all the creamy goodness of ranch with the added benefit of nutrient-dense cashews. Use raw cashews; the roasted ones won't break down, causing your cream base to taste more like a nut butter.

1 cup raw cashews

½ cup cold water, plus more for simmering

1 tablespoon freshly squeezed lemon juice

¾ teaspoon apple cider vinegar

1 teaspoon dried dill

½ teaspoon dried parsle

½ teaspoon dried chives

¼ teaspoon onion powder

½ teaspoon garlic powder

¼ teaspoon table salt

⅛ teaspoon freshly ground black pepper

1. In a small pot, combine the raw cashews with enough water to cover them by 4 inches. Bring to a boil over high heat, then reduce the heat to medium and simmer for 20 minutes. Drain the cashews in a colander, and rinse them under cold running water until they are cool. Transfer the cashews to a blender or food processor, along with the cold water, lemon juice, and apple cider vinegar. Process until smooth, scraping down the sides as needed.

2. In a large measuring cup or small bowl, mix the cashew mixture with the dill, parsley, chives, onion powder, garlic powder, salt, and pepper.

3. The sauce can be used immediately, but for optimal flavor and texture, transfer it to an airtight container and refrigerate for at least 1 hour or, preferably, overnight before using. Store in the refrigerator for up to 1 week.

CHANGE IT UP: If you want a simpler dressing, skip the herbs, onion powder, garlic powder, and pepper.

Per Serving (2 tablespoons): Calories: 53; Fat: 4g; Saturated Fat: 1g; Cholesterol: 0mg; Carbohydrates: 3g; Fiber: 0g; Protein: 2g; Sodium: 30mg

Tempeh "Bacon"

NUT-FREE, 30 MINUTES

SERVES: 4 | **PREP TIME:** 15 minutes | **COOK TIME:** 15 minutes

Tempeh is a protein and nutrient powerhouse. It's made with fermented soybeans that are compressed into a firm block, so, unlike tofu, you get fiber along with protein. Its flavor is neutral, which makes it perfect for adding your own seasonings. This recipe gives you a quick and easy smoky, salty, and sweet sandwich topping, flavorful crumble for a pasta dish, or even a delicious side for pancakes.

1 (8-ounce) package gluten-free tempeh, sliced ¼ inch thick

1 tablespoon smoked paprika

1 teaspoon liquid smoke

½ teaspoon onion powder

¼ cup coconut aminos

2 tablespoons apple cider vinegar

1 cup water

2 tablespoons safflower or avocado oil

2 tablespoons pure maple syrup

1. Line a large nonstick frying pan with the sliced tempeh. Put the pan over medium-high heat and cook until you can hear the tempeh starting to sizzle. Sprinkle the paprika, liquid smoke, and onion powder over the tempeh, then pour in the coconut aminos, apple cider vinegar, and water. Stir gently, bring the liquid to a boil, reduce the heat to medium-low, and cook uncovered for 5 minutes.

2. Add the oil to the pan and gently stir to disperse. Continue to cook, gently flipping the tempeh, until all of the water is gone and the tempeh starts to fry in the oil, about 5 minutes. Cook for about 3 minutes, flipping frequently, until the tempeh has darkened and the edges are crisp. Remove from the heat, pour the maple syrup over the tempeh, flip to coat both sides, and serve.

MAKE AHEAD: You can marinate the seasoned tempeh overnight in the liquid mixture. When you're ready to cook, heat the oil in a nonstick pan over medium-high heat, then carefully place the marinated tempeh in the pan and cook until it is crisp.

Per Serving: Calories: 237; Fat: 13g; Saturated Fat: 2g; Cholesterol: 0mg; Carbohydrates: 15g; Fiber: 1g; Protein: 13g; Sodium: 375mg

Date Caramel Sauce

NUT-FREE, SOY-FREE, 30 MINUTES, CROWD-PLEASER,
WHOLE-FOOD PLANT-BASED

MAKES: 1 pint | **PREP TIME:** 5 minutes | **COOK TIME:** 15 minutes

The base of this four-ingredient caramel sauce is Medjool dates, which have a long list of nutrients, including fiber, potassium, and vitamin B_6. Blend them to make a captivating caramel sauce, and you have a delectable dip for fruit or a tasty topping for pancakes or waffles.

16 pitted Medjool dates

1 cup water

1 teaspoon sea salt

1 teaspoon pure
vanilla extract

¾ to 1 cup unsweetened
gluten-free nondairy milk,
homemade (page 218) or
store-bought

1. In a small saucepan, combine the dates and water. Bring to a boil, reduce the heat to a simmer, and cook for 15 minutes. Add more water as necessary, ¼ cup at a time, so that water is still visible in the pot.

2. Transfer the dates and any liquid to a high-speed blender or food processor, along with the salt, vanilla, and milk. Process until the sauce is smooth, scraping the sides as necessary.

3. Store in an airtight container in the refrigerator for up to 3 weeks.

Per Serving (2 tablespoons) : Calories: 71; Fat: 0g; Saturated Fat: 0g; Cholesterol: 0mg; Carbohydrates: 19g; Fiber: 2g; Protein: 1g; Sodium: 152mg

Enchilada Sauce

ESSENTIAL RECIPE, NUT-FREE, SOY-FREE, 30 MINUTES, CROWD-PLEASER

MAKES: 1 quart | **PREP TIME:** 10 minutes | **COOK TIME:** 10 minutes

The ingredients for this speedy sauce are common pantry items, but the process makes this enchilada sauce unique. The dried spices and tomato paste are cooked in oil, lending it a depth of flavor. The key to success is having all the ingredients nearby; once you start cooking, things move quickly.

1 teaspoon ground cumin

1 teaspoon smoked paprika

½ teaspoon garlic powder

¼ teaspoon dried oregano

¼ teaspoon table salt, plus more to taste

2 tablespoons tomato paste

2 cups low-sodium vegetable stock

3 tablespoons extra-virgin olive oil

3 tablespoons 1:1 all-purpose gluten-free flour, homemade (page 206) or store-bought

1 tablespoon apple cider vinegar

Freshly ground black pepper (optional)

1. In a small bowl, mix the cumin, paprika, garlic powder, oregano, and salt. Measure the tomato paste and stock into separate bowls.

2. In a medium pot, heat the oil over medium heat, then mix in the spices. Stir continuously for 1 minute, then mix in the tomato paste. Cook the tomato paste for 2 minutes, stirring continuously. It should turn dark red in color. Mix in the flour, then cook for 1 minute longer, stirring.

3. Whisk in the vegetable stock, breaking apart any clumps, and bring the mixture to a low simmer. Cook, whisking occasionally, for 5 minutes or until the sauce has thickened a bit. (The sauce will thicken more as it cools.)

4. Remove the pan from the heat, whisk in the vinegar, taste, and add more salt and black pepper if desired. Use immediately, or store the sauce in an airtight container in the refrigerator for up to 3 weeks.

Per Serving (¼ cup): Calories: 31; Fat: 3g; Saturated Fat: 0g; Cholesterol: 0mg; Carbohydrates: 2g; Fiber: 0g; Protein: 0g; Sodium: 38mg

Fresh Berry and Mint Salsa

NUT-FREE, SOY-FREE, 30 MINUTES

MAKES: 3 cups | **PREP TIME:** 20 minutes

When you think of salsa, chances are you think of the standard tomato-based variety. This savory, berry-based salsa is a fresh, antioxidant-rich alternative, and it can be scooped up with chips, spooned over tacos, or even used to top savory and sweet pancakes.

2 cups diced strawberries

½ cup chopped blueberries

½ cup finely diced red onion

½ cup diced red bell pepper

1 jalapeño, seeded and diced

2 teaspoons freshly squeezed lemon juice

2 teaspoons freshly squeezed lime juice

1 teaspoon pure maple syrup

¼ teaspoon table salt

2 tablespoons finely chopped fresh mint

1. In a large bowl, combine the strawberries, blueberries, red onion, bell pepper, and jalapeño. Stir with a heavy wooden spoon, lightly pressing on the berries to release some of their juices and combine their flavors.

2. Stir in the lemon juice, lime juice, maple syrup, salt, and mint. Serve immediately, or refrigerate for 1 hour for best flavor. Store in the refrigerator in an airtight container for up to 2 days.

Per Serving (¼ cup): Calories: 19; Fat: 0g; Saturated Fat: 0g; Cholesterol: 0mg; Carbohydrates: 5g; Fiber: 1g; Protein: 0g; Sodium: 49mg

Sun-Dried-Tomato Ketchup

ESSENTIAL RECIPE, NUT-FREE, SOY-FREE, 30 MINUTES, CROWD-PLEASER

MAKES: 1 quart | **PREP TIME:** 5 minutes | **COOK TIME:** 15 minutes

Ketchup is a popular condiment, but the store-bought varieties are mostly made of refined corn syrup, sugar, and mysterious "natural flavors." Making ketchup at home is a really quick project, and you can control the flavor and the ingredients. This recipe uses sun-dried tomatoes, spices, and vegan Worcestershire sauce to make the best version of this tangy, sweet, and sour condiment.

1 cup apple cider or apple juice

½ cup oil-packed sun-dried tomatoes, drained

¼ cup coconut sugar

¼ cup apple cider vinegar

1 teaspoon vegan Worcestershire sauce

¼ teaspoon ground ginger

⅛ teaspoon ground cloves

⅛ teaspoon cayenne pepper

1 cup diced yellow onion

1 garlic clove, chopped

Table salt

1. In a blender or food processor, combine the apple juice, tomatoes, coconut sugar, vinegar, Worcestershire sauce, ginger, cloves, cayenne pepper, onion, and garlic. Blend until smooth.

2. Transfer the blended mixture to a small saucepan and cook over medium heat for 15 minutes or until it is slightly darkened and thickened. Stir the sauce occasionally to avoid scorching. Add salt to taste. Use the ketchup immediately or store it in an airtight container in the refrigerator for up to 3 weeks (or freeze it for up to 3 months).

INGREDIENT SMARTS: You can use non–oil-packed sun-dried tomatoes for this recipe, but you will need to reconstitute them prior to blending with the other ingredients. Soak the tomatoes in hot water for 30 minutes, drain, and then add them to the blender.

Per Serving (2 tablespoons): Calories: 15; Fat: 0g; Saturated Fat: 0g; Cholesterol: 0mg; Carbohydrates: 3g; Fiber: 0g; Protein: 0g; Sodium: 9mg

Southern-Style Remoulade Sauce

ESSENTIAL RECIPE, NUT-FREE, 30 MINUTES, CROWD-PLEASER

MAKES: 1½ cups | **PREP TIME:** 15 minutes

Remoulade is a French sauce similar to tartar sauce, and this Southern-style version takes it to the next level by adding a little heat. This delicious sauce is a great condiment for fries, burgers, and, of course, the Crispy Hearts of Palm Po' Boy (page 76).

---

1 cup vegan mayo

¼ cup Dijon mustard

1 tablespoon hot sauce (I like Frank's RedHot or Tapatio)

1 garlic clove, minced

2 tablespoons sweet pickle relish

1 tablespoon freshly squeezed lemon juice

1 teaspoon paprika

Table salt

Freshly ground black pepper

---

1. In a medium bowl or dish, whisk together the mayo, mustard, hot sauce, garlic, relish, lemon juice, paprika, salt, and pepper, and gently mash to further combine the relish into the sauce.

2. You can use the sauce immediately or refrigerate it overnight for even more flavor. Store the sauce in an airtight container in the refrigerator for up to 3 weeks. Stir before each serving.

Per Serving (¼ cup): Calories: 144; Fat: 13g; Saturated Fat: 1g; Cholesterol: 0mg; Carbohydrates: 4g; Fiber: 1g; Protein: 3g; Sodium: 506mg

Homemade Nondairy, Gluten-Free Milk

ESSENTIAL RECIPE, SOY-FREE, 30 MINUTES, CROWD-PLEASER, WHOLE-FOOD PLANT-BASED

MAKES: 3½ cups | **PREP TIME:** 10 minutes, plus soaking time

Store-bought nondairy, gluten-free milk comes in so many varieties now, but some have long ingredients lists. Making it at home is relatively easy, and you know exactly what is in it. This recipe gives you three different options for making milk at home using cashews, almonds, or gluten-free oats. These milks can be used interchangeably for any of the recipes in the book, based upon your individual preference.

OAT MILK

1 cup gluten-free oats

4 cups cold water, plus more for soaking

Pinch table salt (optional)

¼ teaspoon xanthan gum (optional)

CASHEW MILK

1 cup raw cashews

4 cups cold water, plus more for soaking

Pinch table salt (optional)

¼ teaspoon xanthan gum (optional)

ALMOND MILK

1 cup raw almonds

4 cups cold water, plus more for soaking

Pinch table salt (optional)

¼ teaspoon xanthan gum (optional)

---

1. To make oat milk: Place the oats in a small bowl, and add enough cold water to just cover the oats. Soak the oats for 10 minutes.

2. To make cashew milk: Place the cashews in a small bowl, and add enough cold water to cover the nuts by 2 inches. Soak the cashews at room temperature for at least 4 hours, preferably overnight.

3. To make almond milk: Place the almonds in a small bowl, and add enough cold water to cover the nuts by 2 inches. Soak the almonds overnight.

4. Drain the oats, cashews, or almonds in a colander, then rinse them under cold running water.

5. Place the oats, cashews, or almonds in a blender; add 4 cups of cold water and the salt and xanthan gum, if using. Blend for 1 minute, then strain the milk through a fine-mesh strainer into a pitcher or large jar. (Keep the remaining pulp to add to other recipes, such as pancakes, waffles, or bread.)

6. Store the milk in an airtight container in the refrigerator for up to 5 days. Shake or stir before each use.

INGREDIENT SMARTS: Oat milk has the least amount of noticeable flavor and is preferred for any savory cream sauce. Almond and cashew milks tend to have hints of natural sweetness that don't translate well in savory sauces. Almond milk has the most flavor, even though it's minimal, and the thinnest consistency.

The optional xanthan gum is flavorless and helps to stabilize the liquid and solids in these milks so they don't separate in the refrigerator. (In other words, if you use xanthan gum, you won't have to shake the milk before using.)

You can turn any of these milks into chocolate milk by blending them with 2 pitted dates, 1 teaspoon of pure vanilla extract, and 2 teaspoons of unsweetened cocoa powder.

Oat Milk Per Serving (1 cup): Calories: 50; Fat: 2g; Saturated Fat: 0g; Cholesterol: 0mg; Carbohydrates: 7g; Fiber: 1g; Protein: 1g; Sodium: 11mg

Cashew Milk Per Serving (1 cup): Calories: 25; Fat: 2g; Saturated Fat: 0g; Cholesterol: 0mg; Carbohydrates: 1g; Fiber: 0g; Protein: 1g; Sodium: 11mg

Almond Milk Per Serving (1 cup): Calories: 30; Fat: 3g; Saturated Fat: 0g; Cholesterol: 0mg; Carbohydrates: 1g; Fiber: 0g; Protein: 1g; Sodium: 10mg

All-Purpose Seasoning

ESSENTIAL RECIPE, NUT-FREE, SOY-FREE, 30 MINUTES, CROWD-PLEASER

MAKES: 1½ cups | **PREP TIME:** 10 minutes

This seasoning blend can be used on just about anything, including oven fries, steamed veggies, tofu scrambles, popcorn, beans and rice, and more. The main benefit of making your own blend is ingredient transparency. Plus, you don't have to worry about potential gluten contamination at the processing facility. This seasoning blend tastes like a cross between taco and Italian seasonings.

¼ cup paprika (or swap in 1 tablespoon of smoked paprika for 1 tablespoon of paprika)

¼ cup sea salt

¼ cup nutritional yeast

2 tablespoons garlic powder

1 tablespoon onion powder

1 tablespoon ground cumin

1 tablespoon vegan sugar (see Ingredient Smarts tip)

2 teaspoons dried basil

2 teaspoons freshly ground black pepper

2 teaspoons tablespoons chili powder

1 teaspoon dried thyme

1 teaspoon celery salt

1. Combine the paprika, salt, nutritional yeast, garlic powder, onion powder, cumin, sugar, basil, pepper, chili powder, thyme, and celery salt in a food processor; pulse 3 or 4 times to combine. The benefit of using a food processor is that you can ensure the ingredients will be fully mixed and any clumps will be broken down.

2. Store the seasoning mixture in an airtight mason jar at room temperature for up to 3 months; the spices will lose their potency after 3 months, but the blend will still be safe to eat.

INGREDIENT SMARTS: Granulated sugar is used intentionally in this recipe. The combination of spices hits nearly all of the flavor categories, and the small amount of sugar gives your tongue just a hint of sweet to balance out the umami, salty, and bitter. Using smoked paprika gives the seasoning a hint of a deeper and more earthy flavor, but it is a personal preference.

Per Serving (1 teaspoon): Calories: 5; Fat: 0g; Saturated Fat: 0g; Cholesterol: 0mg; Carbohydrates: 1g; Fiber: 0g; Protein: 0g; Sodium: 425mg

Buffalo Sauce

NUT-FREE, SOY-FREE, 30 MINUTES, CROWD-PLEASER

MAKES: 2½ cups | **PREP TIME:** 10 minutes | **COOK TIME:** 7 minutes

It is nearly impossible to find vegan Buffalo sauce at the grocery store, but with only a few ingredients and about 15 minutes, you can make your own version of this rich and spicy sauce, ready for burgers, fries, and just about anything that needs a little heat. Don't be scared by the amount of butter in this recipe; it is spread (excuse the pun) across about 40 (1-tablespoon) servings.

1½ cups Frank's RedHot sauce or other cayenne pepper hot sauce

1 cup vegan butter

3 tablespoons white vinegar

½ teaspoon vegan Worcestershire sauce

½ teaspoon garlic powder

1 teaspoon paprika

---

1. In a small pot, combine the hot sauce, butter, vinegar, Worcestershire sauce, garlic powder, and paprika and bring the mixture to a boil, stirring occasionally. (Caution: When boiling anything with a lot of pepper, make sure not to put your face near the top of the pot. The spicy steam can sting!) Reduce the heat to low and cook for 5 minutes, until the sauce is bubbling around the edges.

2. Store the sauce in a sealed jar in the refrigerator for up to 1 month. The butter in this sauce will firm up when cooled. Reheat the sauce to thin it, or serve it thick from the jar.

INGREDIENT SMARTS: The recipe calls for Frank's RedHot sauce because it is common in grocery stores, affordable, vegan, and gluten-free. Some hot sauces contain wheat thickeners or so-called natural flavors that aren't vegan.

Per Serving (1 tablespoon): Calories: 5; Fat: 0g; Saturated Fat: 0g; Cholesterol: 0mg; Carbohydrates: 1g; Fiber: 0g; Protein: 0g; Sodium: 425mg

Mojo Sauce

ESSENTIAL RECIPE, NUT-FREE, SOY-FREE, 30 MINUTES, CROWD-PLEASER

MAKES: 1 pint | **PREP TIME:** 15 minutes

There are as many versions of mojo sauce as there are salsas. This Cuban-style version gets its flavor from earthy spices combined with sweet-and-sour orange juice. Feel free to use this sauce as a marinade for jackfruit or soy curls, or as a topping for fresh or roasted veggies.

Zest and juice of 1 large navel orange

Juice of 2 limes

1 jalapeño, halved, and seeded

2 garlic cloves

½ cup chopped fresh cilantro

¼ cup extra-virgin olive oil

2 teaspoons coconut sugar

1 teaspoon kosher salt

In a blender or food processor, combine the orange, lime juice, jalapeño, garlic, cilantro, oil, coconut sugar, and salt and puree until smooth. Store in an airtight container in the refrigerator for up to 1 week.

Per Serving (2 tablespoons): Calories: 37; Fat: 3g; Saturated Fat: 0g; Cholesterol: 0mg; Carbohydrates: 2g; Fiber: 0g; Protein: 0g; Sodium: 102mg

Basic Vinaigrette and Variations

NUT-FREE, SOY-FREE, 30 MINUTES, CROWD-PLEASER

MAKES: 1 cup | **PREP TIME:** 5 minutes

Whether you're throwing a dinner party or making a quick salad for one, it's handy to have some vinaigrette at the ready. Vinaigrette is essentially three components: oil, vinegar, and an emulsifier to keep the two liquids together. Beyond that, there are endless ways to change it up. Here are a few varieties, but once you grasp the basics, you can make your own vinaigrette creations.

½ cup extra-virgin olive oil

¼ cup red wine vinegar

1 tablespoon Dijon mustard

1 tablespoon pure maple syrup

2 garlic cloves, pressed or crushed, then minced

¼ teaspoon fine sea salt

¼ teaspoon freshly ground black pepper

1. In a pint-size mason jar, combine the oil, vinegar, mustard, maple syrup, garlic, salt, and pepper. Seal the lid and shake to combine.

2. Serve immediately, or seal and refrigerate for up to 1 month. When the oil is cold, your vinaigrette might appear thick and cloudy. Allow it to warm up at room temperature for 1 hour before using, or run hot water over the jar for a few minutes.

CHANGE IT UP: Balsamic Vinaigrette: Swap the red wine vinegar for balsamic to make a bold and slightly sweet dressing that pairs wonderfully with a salad made of bitter greens, chopped walnuts, and chopped apples or stone fruits.

ITALIAN VINAIGRETTE: Add 1 teaspoon dried oregano and 1 teaspoon Italian seasoning. Use the red wine vinegar as stated in the recipe, or swap it out for white wine vinegar.

RASPBERRY VINAIGRETTE: Mash 1 cup fresh or frozen and thawed raspberries, then mix them into the vinaigrette along with 2 tablespoons finely minced shallot.

Per Serving (2 tablespoons): Calories: 130; Fat: 14g; Saturated Fat: 2g; Cholesterol: 0mg; Carbohydrates: 2g; Fiber: 0g; Protein: 0g; Sodium: 95mg

Menus for Any Occasion

ITALIAN-THEMED DINNER PARTY

APPETIZERS: Amaranth and Walnut Pilaf (page 108), Smoky Tempeh-Stuffed Mushrooms (page 52)

SOUP AND SALAD: Peach and Basil Caprese Salad (page 72), Creamy Zuppa Toscana (page 88)

MAIN DISH AND SIDE: Edamame Pesto Pasta (page 132), Brussels Sprout Slaw (page 97)

DESSERT: Flourless Chocolate Cake (page 176)

VEGAN JUNK FOOD FEST

APPETIZERS: Panko Jalapeño Poppers (page 56), Corn Dog–Style Baby Carrots (page 58), Soft Pretzel Bites with Beer Cheese (page 66)

MAIN DISHES: Buffalo Chickpea Sliders (page 122), BBQ Soy Curl Hoagies (page 128), Chili Mac and Cheese (page 154)

DESSERT: No-Bake Caramel Brownie Bars (page 196)

TABLE TOPPERS: Sun-Dried-Tomato Ketchup (page 216), BBQ Sauce (page 207), Buffalo Sauce (page 221)

FANCY DINNER DATE OR PARTY

APPETIZER AND SOUP: Balsamic Mushroom and Quinoa Lettuce Wraps (page 81), Roasted Butternut Squash Soup (page 92)

MAIN DISH AND SIDE: Zucchini Lasagna Pockets (page 168), Roasted Carrots and Fennel (page 110)

DESSERT: Peach and Blueberry Galette (page 192)

PICNIC MENU

SNACKS AND DRINK: Tahini and Seeds Granola Bars (page 49), Pineapple-Turmeric-Ginger Lemonade (page 62)

MAIN DISH: Sunflower Seed "Tuna" Sandwiches (page 74) on Seeded Sandwich Bread (page 200)

DESSERT: Chocolate Dessert Hummus (page 209) with apple slices

KID FAVORITES

BREAKFAST: Fluffy Pancakes (page 25) with Chocolate Dessert Hummus (page 209) and fresh berries

SNACK: Tahini and Seeds Granola Bars (page 49)

LUNCH: Tofu Nuggets (page 50) with Sun-Dried-Tomato Ketchup (page 216)

DINNER: Cauliflower and Sweet Potato Crust Pizzas (page 148)

DESSERT: Apple Cider Muffins (page 186)

THE "NO TIME" DAY

BREAKFAST: Chickpea Flour Granola (page 30) with nondairy yogurt and fresh blueberries

SNACK: Candied Coconut Cashews (page 54) and a banana

LUNCH: Chickpea Caesar Salad Wrap (page 75)

DINNER: Quick Pad Thai (page 142)

DESSERT: Chocolate Mug Cake (page 178)

Burger Buns, >
page **202**

Measurement Conversions

	US STANDARD	US STANDARD (OUNCES)	METRIC (APPROXIMATE)
VOLUME EQUIVALENTS (LIQUID)	2 tablespoons	1 fl. oz.	30 mL
	¼ cup	2 fl. oz.	60 mL
	½ cup	4 fl. oz.	120 mL
	1 cup	8 fl. oz.	240 mL
	1½ cups	12 fl. oz.	355 mL
	2 cups or 1 pint	16 fl. oz.	475 mL
	4 cups or 1 quart	32 fl. oz.	1 L
	1 gallon	128 fl. oz.	4 L
VOLUME EQUIVALENTS (DRY)	⅛ teaspoon	——	0.5 mL
	¼ teaspoon	——	1 mL
	½ teaspoon	——	2 mL
	¾ teaspoon	——	4 mL
	1 teaspoon	——	5 mL
	1 tablespoon	——	15 mL
	¼ cup	——	59 mL
	⅓ cup	——	79 mL
	½ cup	——	118 mL
	⅔ cup	——	156 mL
	¾ cup	——	177 mL
	1 cup	——	235 mL
	2 cups or 1 pint	——	475 mL
	3 cups	——	700 mL
	4 cups or 1 quart	——	1 L
	½ gallon	——	2 L
	1 gallon	——	4 L
WEIGHT EQUIVALENTS	½ ounce	——	15 g
	1 ounce	——	30 g
	2 ounces	——	60 g
	4 ounces	——	115 g
	8 ounces	——	225 g
	12 ounces	——	340 g
	16 ounces or 1 pound	——	455 g

	FAHRENHEIT (F)	CELSIUS (C) (APPROXIMATE)
OVEN TEMPERATURES	250°F	120°C
	300°F	150°C
	325°F	180°C
	375°F	190°C
	400°F	200°C
	425°F	220°C
	450°F	230°C

Resources

EAT RIGHT, ACADEMY OF NUTRITION AND DIETETICS (EatRight.org)
The Academy of Nutrition and Dietetics is the world's largest organization of food and nutrition professionals, and their website offers nutrition support and articles on how to best benefit from the nutrition of a plant-based diet.

FORKS OVER KNIVES (ForksOverKnives.com)
This is my favorite online resource for recipe ideas, vegan cooking techniques, and beautiful food photography. They have a monthly magazine and cookbooks, and they post daily on social media. All of their recipes are vegan, and some are also gluten-free.

THE HOW NOT TO DIE COOKBOOK: 100 + RECIPES TO HELP PREVENT AND REVERSE DISEASE, by Michael Greger and Gene Stone
This research-based book gives information on how to prevent and fight specific diseases with plant-based recipes. This is a great resource to have in your cookbook collection as you learn more about a plant-based diet.

"PLANT-BASED DIETS ARE ASSOCIATED WITH A LOWER RISK OF INCIDENT CARDIOVASCULAR DISEASE," published by Hyunju Kim, et al. *Journal of the American Heart Association* 8, no. 16 (2019). doi: 10.1161/JAHA.119.012865.
If you want to learn more about how eating a plant-based diet affects your cardiovascular health, this article gives you a lot of information.

MAYO CLINIC GOING GLUTEN-FREE: ESSENTIAL GUIDE TO MANAGING CELIAC DISEASE AND RELATED CONDITIONS, by Joseph A. Murray M.D.
If you are new to a gluten-free diet, you'll appreciate the advice, strategies, and medical perspectives found in this book. It offers information about common triggers, hidden foods with gluten, and ways to manage symptoms of gluten allergies and intolerance.

Index

About the Author

JUSTIN WEBER is from northern Wisconsin, has two children who give him the "Yum" or "Yuck" on recipes, and posts recipes and health tips on social media using the handle @CrowMoonKitchen.

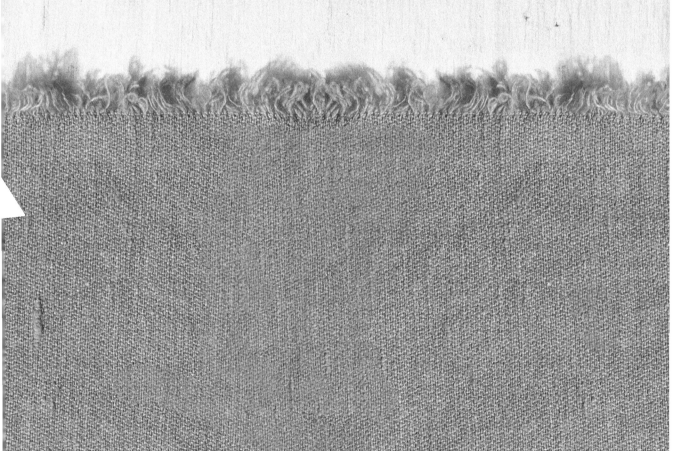

Printed in the USA
CPSIA information can be obtained
at www.ICGtesting.com
LVHW060025050124
767685LV00003B/12